Hugh Stoker

Sea Fishing in Dorset

with sketch charts and tackle illustrations by the author

Mill House Publications,
The Mill House, Seatown, Bridport, Dorset.

Tel: (0297) 89756

By the same author:

THE MODERN SEA ANGLER
SEA ANGLING HOTSPOTS
A MANUAL OF SEA FISHING BAITS
SEA ANGLING WITH THE SPECIMEN HUNTERS
SEA FISHING IN HAMPSHIRE & ISLE OF WIGHT
WEST DORSET WALKS
SOUTH DORSET WALKS
EAST DEVON WALKS

First Published 1960
Second impression (revised) 1963
Third impression (revised) 1967
Fourth impression (revised) 1972
Fifth impression (revised) 1977
Sixth impression (revised) 1986
Seventh impression (revised) 1989
Eighth impression (revised) 1993

ISBN 0 9508088 3 0

CONTENTS

Page

Author's Note 4

Hints for Beginners
This section includes information on shore and boat fishing methods, terminal tackle rigs, knots, etc. 5

Some Fish Worth Catching and How to Catch Them 12

Fishing Areas . . .

Mudeford (*with Highcliff and Christchurch Harbour*) 23

Bournemouth (*with Southbourne and Boscombe*) 28

Poole Harbour 32

Studland 39

Swanage 40

Chapman's Pool 44

Kimmeridge Bay 47

Lulworth Cove 50

Weymouth and Portland 56

Chesil Beach (*with Abbotsbury, Bexington, Swyre and Burton Bradstock*) 68

Bridport (*West Bay and Eype*) 71

Seatown 75

Charmouth 79

Lyme Regis 81

Author's Note

THIS book is the result of many years of sea angling and wandering in small craft along the Dorset coast. Every place mentioned in the following pages has been visited personally, and both shore and boat fishing marks have been put to the test.

Even so, this book could never have been made so comprehensive without the friendly help of hundreds of other Dorset sea fishermen, and I take this opportunity of thanking all who placed so much of their local knowledge at my disposal.

Of course, local changes are bound to occur. Boatmen and tackle dealers come and go, and sometimes shore fishing positions become affected by coast erosion. In this new edition, a great many revisions have been made, and in addition mention has been made of newly discovered marks and fishing techniques. Naturally I shall do my best to keep this book up to date when printing future editions, and anglers are welcome to co-operate by reporting any local changes of this nature.

Tide tables have not been included with this book because they would soon have become out-of-date. However, tidal constants are quoted throughout with reference to High Water London Bridge—the times of which are quoted in most daily papers.

Finally, I would like to state that while every effort has been made to ensure the accuracy of tidal and other navigational information included in this book, no responsibility can be accepted for any errors or omissions which may have escaped notice. It should be noted also that tidal streams shown on the charts are liable to be affected by weather conditions, estuary currents, or the configuration of coastline and sea-bed.

HUGH STOKER

Hints for Beginners

FISHING FROM PIERS AND HARBOUR BREAKWATERS. For the beginner, who has yet to master the art of casting long distances, a pier or harbour breakwater provides an easy means of getting the baited tackle into reasonably deep water. Indeed, long casting can very often be a disadvantage when pier fishing, because several species of fish spend most of their time close to the seaweedy piles or masonry.

Therein lies a difficulty, because fighting kinds of fish – such as bass, mackerel, pollack and mullet – will probably try to gain the safety of the piles as soon as they are hooked. To steer them clear, a reasonably firm (but not rigid) rod may be desirable. It should not be too long, however; otherwise it will be awkward to handle on a crowded pier. Many anglers who specialize in this sort of fishing use a rod about 8 to 9ft long, matched with a medium-sized fixed spool reel or multiplier.

There is no need to use the old-fashioned 'barge-pole' type of pier rod. When a fish of above-average size is hooked, it is usually possible to lift it out of the water with the aid of a drop-net. This is a bag-shaped net lashed to an iron hoop or old bicycle wheel rim, which can be lowered from the pier by means of a rope and bridle.

The methods most commonly used from a pier or harbour breakwater are bottom fishing and float fishing.

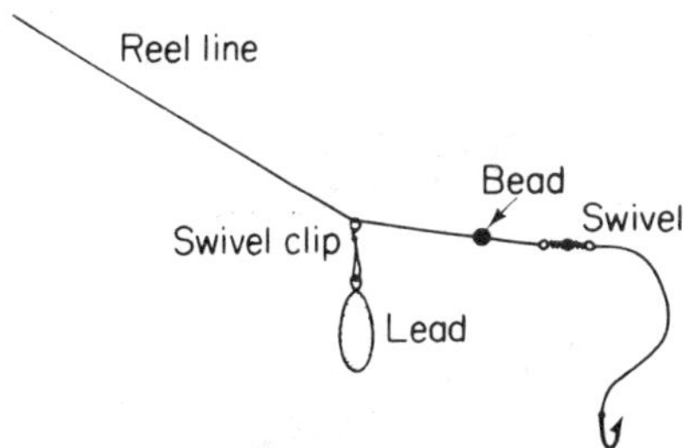

Fig. 1 Leger rig

There are many different kinds of bottom tackle, but the types known as paternoster, paternoster-trot and leger will meet most requirements when ground fishing from a pier. They are all illustrated in this section, and can be made up at home out of nylon monofilament. It is important, though, to use the right knots for this job.

The paternoster is a good general purpose rig, and it can either be cast out and left lying on the sea-bed, or suspended on

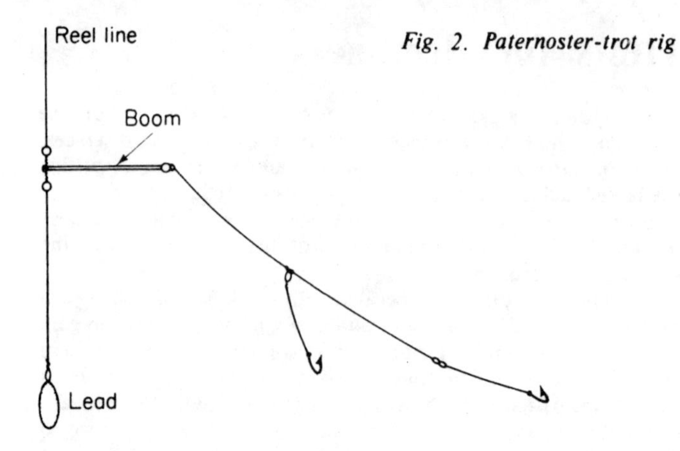

Fig. 2. Paternoster-trot rig

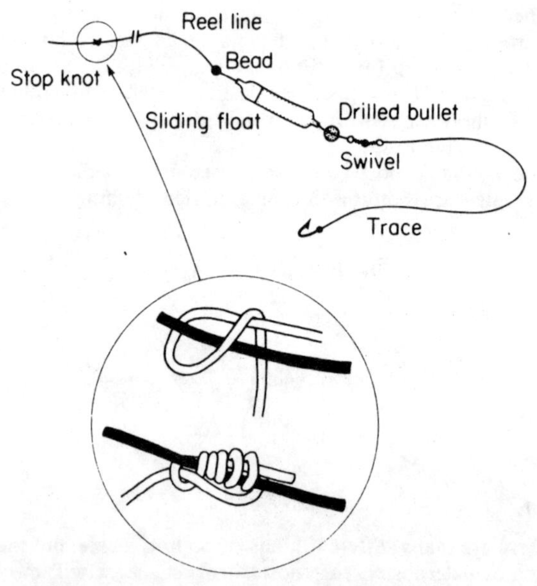

Fig. 3 Sliding float tackle. The trace should have a slightly lower breaking strain than the reel line

a tight-line. In the latter case a position about 6 inches to 2 feet above the sea-bed usually gives good results, especially when the bottom is rocky or weedy.

Float tackle is normally used to catch those fish which swim between mid-water and the surface, such as bass, mackerel, scad and garfish. However, when the water is fairly shallow, float tackle can also be adjusted to catch pollack, wrasse, flounders and other species which normally swim quite near the bottom. This is useful in areas where crabs are quick to attack baits fished right on the bottom.

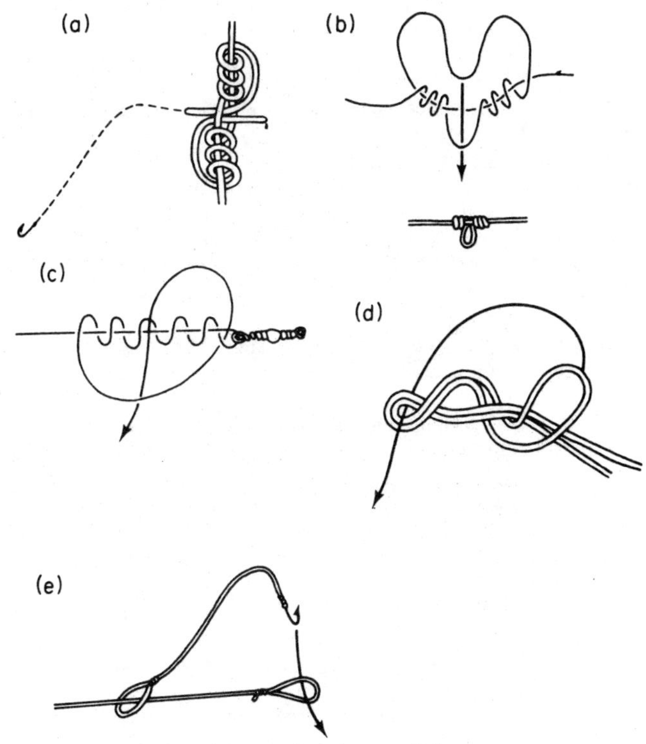

Fig. 4 A variety of knots for the sea fisherman
- *(a) Blood knot, which is primarily for joining two lines of similar diameter, but can be employed as a hook dropper by leaving one end long*
- *(b) Paternoster blood loop – for attaching a hook dropper link to the main line*
- *(c) Half-blood clinch knot*
- *(d) Blood bight knot (to form a looped end)*
- *(e) How to join two looped ends*

When float fishing at a depth greater than the length of your rod, it is necessary to use a sliding float. The reason for this, of course, is that a fixed float would jam against the end-ring of the rod when reeling in, leaving a hooked fish dangling out of reach, or still swimming around in the sea. A sliding float, on the other hand, slips down the line when taken out of the water, and comes to rest just above the lead. This makes retrieving and casting quite easy.

As soon as the float alights on the water after casting it slides up the line until checked by a small 'stop knot' tied from a few inches of nylon line. This stop knot can be slid up or down the reel line as desired, and by adjusting its position you can control the fishing depth.

Harbour breakwaters and quays are often the haunt of large mullet, and these can provide excellent sport on light float tackle. The best time to try for these fish is very early in the morning, before boats and holidaymakers are on the move. It is essential to fish quietly and unobtrusively, and to groundbait the swim at frequent intervals – preferably with sopped bread.

Tackle for harbour mullet comprises a light quill float, 5lb line, a freshwater-type rod and fixed-spool reel, using a size 8 to 12 hook baited with bread flake, crust or paste, tiny harbour ragworm, maggots, pork fat, etc. A landing net is essential for this species, because a mullet's mouth is soft and the hook will pull out very easily.

If you are keen to catch a really big fish, it is worth bearing in mind that old crevice-filled harbour walls are often inhabited by large conger eels. These provide exciting sport – especially at night – for anyone equipped with a strong rod and reel. For bait you can use a big cutting of mackerel or squid on a large hook. Leger tackle is best, and it should be fitted with a strong link-swivel. It is also advisable to have a few inches of wire next to the hook, because conger have sharp teeth and very powerful jaws.

For the same reason, when you have caught a conger, keep your fingers away from its mouth, and don't try to remove the hook. Instead, unclip the trace from the link-swivel, and fit another.

ROCK FISHING is very similar to pier fishing. If anything it is more pleasant, because you will probably be much closer to the water and fishing under less crowded conditions. This opens up possibilities for spinning with an artificial lure or suitable natural bait such as a small fresh sandeel. The fish taken on spinning tackle include bass, pollack, mackerel and garfish. The favourite local artificial spinning lures are described later in this book.

Float fishing is another popular rock fishing method which also accounts for bass, pollack, mackerel and garfish, together with wrasse and pouting when the float is set to fish the bait near the bottom.

Where the sea-bed is very snaggy it may be impossible to use bottom fishing tactics from a rock position, but quite often a preliminary survey at low tide will reveal patches of snag-free sand where it would be possible to cast out a simple paternoster or leger trace. This sort of ground often produces sizeable bass, conger, huss, wrasse and, in some areas, large thornback rays.

BEACH FISHING is one of the most interesting forms of sea angling, but as a general rule one must possess the necessary skill and tackle to cast the bait out a fair distance. One possible exception is the type of shingle beach which shelves steeply into fairly deep water. On this sort of shoreline a very modest cast of only 30 to 40 yards is often sufficient to place the bait among the feeding fish, especially when fishing after dark when most fish tend to move closer inshore.

At the other extreme is the gently shelving ocean-facing storm beach, where a spectacular run of surf comes roaring and creaming up the sand. This type of fishing mark can provide excellent sport with bass, but the ability to cast out a good distance (say 80 to 100 yards plus) is more or less essential.

Fig. 5. Shorecasting paternoster (type of lead is optional).

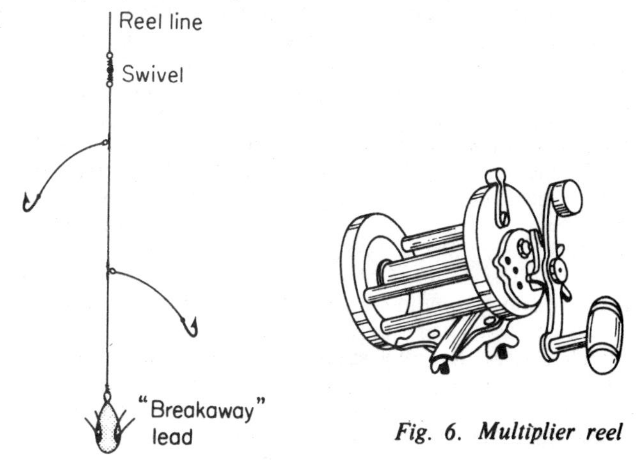

Fig. 6. Multiplier reel

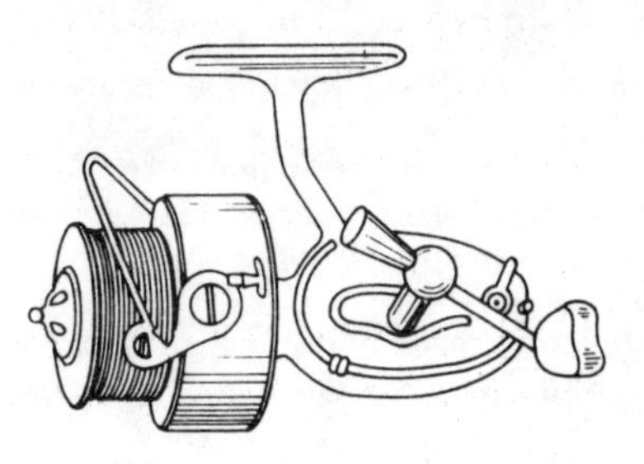

Fig. 7. Fixed-spool reel

The rod for distance beachcasting should be about 11 to 12ft in length, with a good brisk action, and balanced by a reel of adequate line capacity – say 200 yards or more. Various kinds of reel are used, including multipliers, large and medium-sized fixed-spools, and side-casters. For the novice, a fixed-spool reel is almost certainly the best choice, as this type is easier to handle than a multiplier – especially when fishing at night.

Most expert long-distance surfcasters, on the other hand, prefer to use a multiplier reel.

The breaking strain of your reel line will depend partly on the power of the rod, and partly on the local shore conditions. Where snaggy rocks abound, or where the angler has to contend with trailing masses of kelp, it is inevitable that a heavy line and powerful rod will have to be used.

However, such conditions are the exception rather than the rule, and normally it is possible to load a shorecasting reel with line in the 17 to 22lb breaking strain range. It is important to remember that the finer the line the less resistance it offers to the flying lead and bait when casting, and this results in greater distances.

When using a light line, however, it is absolutely essential to tie an 18ft length of stronger 30lb b.s. line to the end of the reel line. This is known as a 'shock leader', and its purpose is to absorb the sudden stress which occurs during the moment of casting. Incidentally, if you are casting with a lead weighing in excess of the customary 4oz size, you will need to use a proportionately stronger shock leader.

Your choice of terminal trace for beachcasting will depend largely on local conditions, and elsewhere in this book, when discussing individual shore marks, I have listed the most suitable traces. Generally speaking, however, these are usually variations on the monofil paternoster, paternoster-trot and running leger theme, with paternoster rigs the hot favourite in areas where snaggy conditions prevail.

BOAT ANGLING offers a very wide choice of fishing methods. At anchor, you can fish on the bottom (assuming that it is not too snaggy) with a paternoster, leger or paternoster-trot. You can also fish above the bottom (or any other desired depth) with a driftline or tight-lined paternoster. For this sort of general sea fishing it is best to use a short-butted medium-powered glass-fibre boat rod, about 6½ to 7ft in length. This should be matched with a medium-sized boat fishing multiplier reel, loaded with line of about 30 to 35lb breaking strain. The actual choice between nylon monofilament line and braided terylene is very much a matter of personal choice, but it is worth mentioning that nylon monofilament is a good deal cheaper, and offers less water resistance – an important factor in areas where tides run fast.

Trolling is another rewarding boat fishing method. For this the boat is kept on the move, either by oars, motor or sail, and an artificial lure or natural bait trailed astern. Mackerel, pollack, bass and garfish are commonly taken in this way, although the terminal tackle, lure, fishing depth and speed of the boat must be varied to suit the species.

As a rough guide, mackerel are widespread and found in a very wide range of depths; garfish are more likely to be encountered fairly near the surface; pollack are found fairly deep near reefs and rocky headlands, except around dawn and evening when they often rise towards the surface; and bass are mostly encountered near river estuaries, surf-whitened shoals, or inshore rocks.

There are specialist forms of boat angling which call for somewhat heavier tackle – notably deep-sea wreck fishing for giant conger and ling. For this sort of fishing a powerful rod is required, matched with a big-game type multiplier reel loaded with line of not less than 50lb breaking strain.

At the other end of the scale there will be many inshore dinghy anglers who prefer to fish with light, sporting tackle. One recommended method is float fishing for bass in shallow rocky coves, or in the vicinity of sandeel-inhabited sandbars. Light driftlining, using the tidal current to stream the bait above the bottom, is another favourite method. For this sort of fishing live prawns and live sandeels are both excellent.

* * *

Some Fish Worth Catching and How to Catch Them

The following is a list of the more sporting sea fish commonly caught on rod and line. Although we have quoted the times of year when each species is most likely to be encountered, it must be stressed that these periods should only be regarded as a rough guide. Fish are influenced by water temperature, food supply and various other factors, and their movements usually vary slightly from year to year.

BASS

Coloration: Bluish-grey above; silvery on sides and white underneath. Dark lateral line.
Season: Present inshore from late spring to about November or December.
Habitat: Generally found in the vicinity of inshore reefs, rocky headlands, sandbars and tidal estuaries.

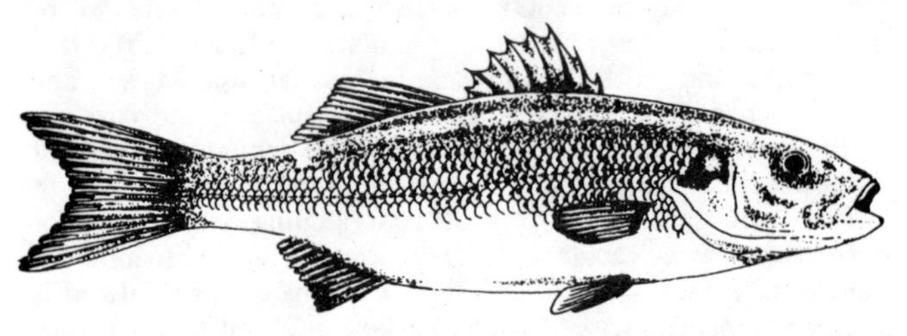

Shore Fishing Methods: (i) Surfcasting with bottom tackle; (ii) Float fishing from rocks, piers, harbour walls, etc.; (iii) Spinning from rocks, steeply shelving beach or estuary sand-spit.

Boat Fishing Methods: (i) Spinning from a drifting dinghy; (ii) Trolling with a natural or artificial bait; (iii) Driftlining from an anchored boat; (iv) Float fishing in a shallow cove.
Baits: Sandeels, prawns, peeler and soft crab, lugworm, ragworm, squid, mackerel strips.

BREAM

Two species of sea bream inhabit British waters, the Red Bream and the Black Bream. In both cases the larger fish are mostly taken by boat anglers.

Coloration: Red Bream – brownish-scarlet on the back, shading to reddish-silver on the sides and belly. Adult fish have a dark patch on the shoulder. Black Bream – variable but generally bluish-grey above, shading to silvery-grey on the sides.
Season: Early summer to mid-autumn.
Habitat: Both red and black bream favour areas of weedy rock or rough ground, and sunken weedy wrecks. They are usually found fairly near the bottom.

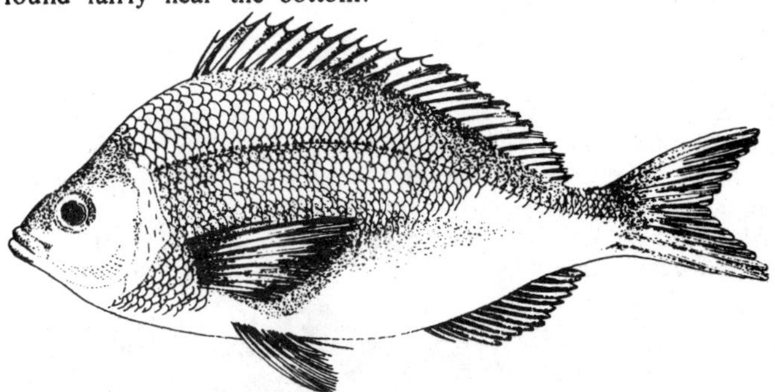

Fishing Methods: Although red and black bream are both occasionally caught from the shore, the majority of fish caught in this way are rather small. For the most part, therefore, bream fishing is carried on from boats, using light driftline tackle and a single size 6 hook on a flowing trace.
Baits: Tiny strips of squid, mackerel or herring; lugworm, ragworm or mussel.

COD

Coloration: Variable, but generally a mottled or marbled sandy-brown on the back and sides. Curved white lateral line and white belly. Cod from kelpy areas are often a coppery-red hue, with darker spots.
Season: Inshore cod fishing is at its best from about November to February, but some big cod are also caught in summer from deepwater wrecks and similar offshore marks.
Habitat: A bottom feeder, favouring sandy or broken grounds; also areas of kelp and rock on some coasts.

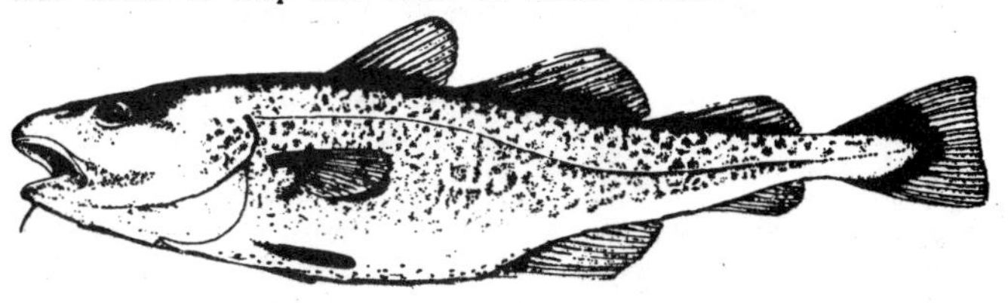

Shore Fishing Methods: Bottom fishing from a steep-to beach or pier, using large hooks and baits.
Boat Fishing Methods: Paternoster, paternoster-trot or driftline fished on or just above the bottom.
Baits: Squid, lugworms, mussels, mackerel and herring strips, etc.

CONGER

Coloration: Dark sooty brown on back, shading to greyish-white underneath.
Season: From about late spring to early winter inshore; all the year round from deepwater marks.
Habitat: Lives on the bottom amongst crevice-filled rocks, sunken wrecks and underwater caverns.
Shore Fishing Method: Leger tackle cast out on to snag-free ground close to rocks or a sea-eroded stone harbour wall.

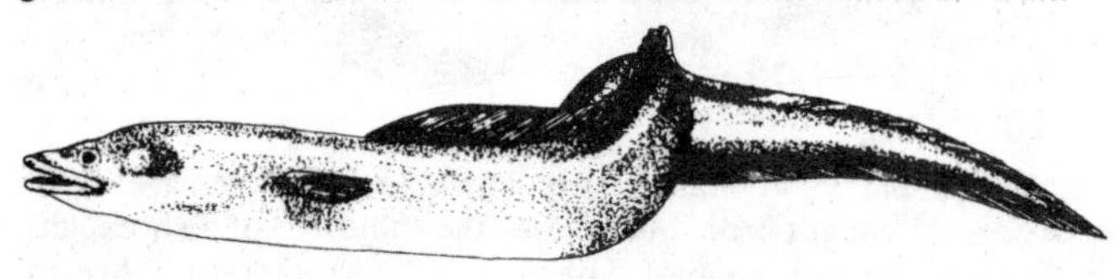

Boat Fishing Methods: Leger tackle streamed down to a suitable rock mark or sunken wreck. Strong tackle is essential for the big ones, and owing to the conger's sharp teeth it is essential to fit a few inches of flexible cable-laid stainless steel wire next to the hook.
Baits: Large offerings of squid, mackerel, herring; small whole pouting, wrasse, etc.

DABS

Coloration: These small but very tasty flatfish are light sandy brown on the upper side; white underneath.
Season: From early summer to late winter.
Habitat: Areas of fine sand or muddy sand.
Shore and Boat Fishing: Light nylon paternoster or leger fitted with small hooks – say about size 6 or 8, depending on bait used.
Baits: Ragworm, lugworm, mussel, razorfish, squid tentacle.

FLOUNDERS

Coloration: Varies from a sandy brown to very dark muddy brown on the back; white underneath.

Season: From late spring to late winter.
Habitat: These medium-sized flatfish are usually found in or near tidal estuaries where the bottom is sand or mud.
Shore Fishing Methods: (i) Light nylon paternoster or leger; (ii) Spinning with a baited-spoon.
Boat Fishing Methods: (i) Light nylon leger or paternoster; (ii) Dinghy trolling with oars and a baited-spoon.
Baits: Ragworm, lugworm, peeler crab and slipper limpet.

GARFISH

Coloration: This strange-looking beaked fish is bluish-green on the back, shading to silver on the belly. It has green bones but don't let this put you off – it is quite safe to eat!

Season: Late spring to early autumn.
Habitat: Nomadic, often feeding fairly near the surface on small fry.
Shore Fishing Methods: (i) Spinning with small shiny artificial lures; (ii) Float fishing.
Baits: Tiny strips of mackerel or other garfish.

MACKEREL

Coloration: Scribbled wavy black markings on the back against a background of brilliant green or blue, shading to a silvery belly. The lateral line is a thin seam of black.
Season: In inshore waters the mackerel shoals are present from about May to October, but there are wide regional variations.
Habitat: Nomadic and swims in large shoals, sometimes very close inshore and sometimes far out to sea. Feeds largely on whitebait and other small fry, including sandeels, at widely varying depths from the surface to over 50 fathoms.

Shore Fishing Methods: (i) Spinning with small artificial lures; (ii) Light float fishing; (iii) Casting out and retrieving a feathered mackerel trace.
Boat Fishing Methods: (i) Spinning with small artificial lures; (ii) Trolling with small artificial lures; (iii) Jigging with a trace of mackerel feathers; (iv) Light float fishing.
Baits: Small strips of mackerel flesh; a whole small sandeel, preferably live.

MULLET, GREY

Coloration: Bluish-grey on the back, shading to silvery underneath, with darker longitudinal bars along the sides. There are three British species of grey mullet, but the thick-lipped grey mullet is the most common one, and attains the largest size.

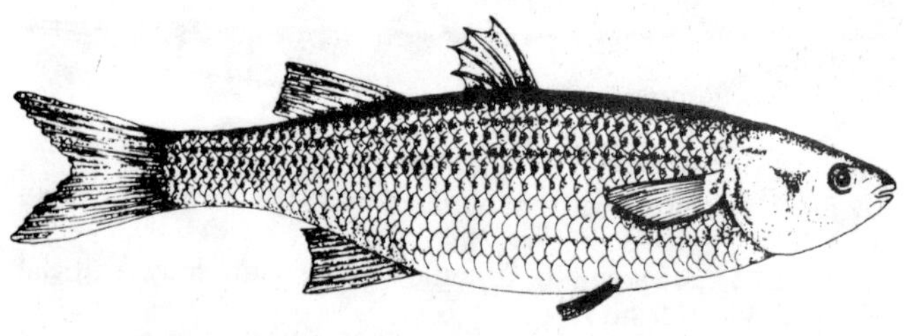

Season: Summer and early autumn.
Habitat: Tidal estuaries, harbours and on the open coast, especially near rocky headlands.
Fishing Methods: Mullet fishing is nearly always carried on from shore positions, such as harbour walls, piers, rock ledges, etc. The most common method is to use light freshwater-type float tackle, and as mullet fishing is a very specialised form of sea angling the following hints may prove helpful:

Before tackling up, groundbait the swim to attract the mullet and get them feeding. This is most important. Sopped bread is often used for this purpose, but in a fishing harbour where the mullet are used to feeding on galley scraps and discarded fish scraps, it is worth offering them some mackerel guts and ray's liver, chopped up fine.

When fishing in a sheltered harbour I usually tackle up with a small quill float, but in more open water I use a small cork-bodied Avon float. The line should be as light as local conditions permit – say about 5lb b.s. Use a tiny hook, about size 10 or 12. Position the split shot fairly near the float so that the baited hook drifts in advance. A good distance between the hook-eye and float-eye is about 18 inches – although naturally this only applies when the fish are feeding near the surface, and in any case it pays to experiment. Avoid slack line; keep quiet and out of sight of the fish as much as possible, avoiding any unnecessary movement. Strike promptly, but not too vigorously. Play the fish carefully, and if fishing from a harbour wall have a roomy drop-net already in the water a few yards down-tide from your swim. Play your fish away from the shoal towards the waiting net, so as to avoid scaring the other fish.

Fish that are to be returned to the water should be placed in a keep-net, and given their freedom at the *end* of your fishing session. Fish liberated during a fishing session are likely to take the remainder of the shoal with them.

Baits: The best all-round bait for mullet is bread, either flake, crust or paste, and it has the added advantage of appealing only to mullet, so that you will not be pestered with small pollack, pouting, etc. However, in some commercial fishing harbours you may achieve better results with tiny slips of mackerel or pilchard flesh. Other baits worth a trial are small harbour ragworm, bacon fat, maggots and cheese.

PLAICE

Coloration: Variable, but usually brownish or greenish-brown on the upper side with some orange or red spots; white underneath.

Season: Early summer to mid-winter, depending on locality.

Habitat: Lives on the bottom in areas of firm sand, shell-grit or muddy sand, where it feeds on marine worms, burrowing molluscs and shrimps.

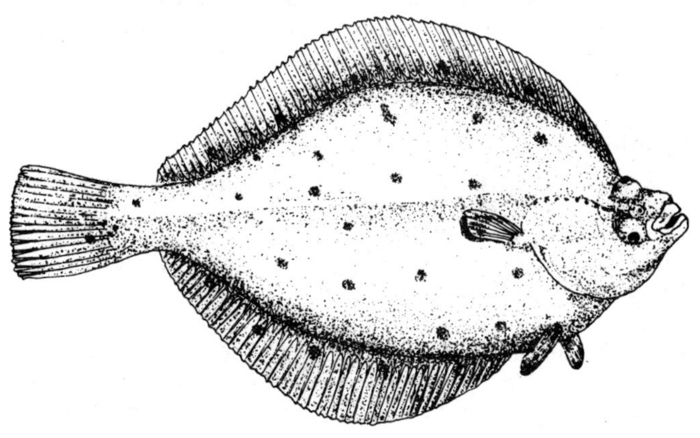

Shore and Boat Fishing Methods: Bottom fishing with a light nylon paternoster-trot or leger, using hooks up to about size 2/0, depending on bait used and average size of fish in locality. Plaice, like flounders, can also be taken on a baited-spoon.
Baits: Ragworm, razorfish, lugworm, cockle, mussel, etc.

POLLACK

Coloration: Varies according to locality, but generally reddish-brown or greenish-bronze on the back, shading to white underneath. The lateral line is darker than its background – a feature which immediately distinguishes it from its near relative, the coalfish, which has a white lateral line against a dark background.
Season: From about April to late autumn inshore, and well into winter in deep water.
Habitat: Weedy reefs, deepwater rocks and sunken wrecks.
Shore Fishing Methods: (i) Spinning with an artificial plastic sandeel or metal wobbling spoon; (ii) Float fishing from a rock position.

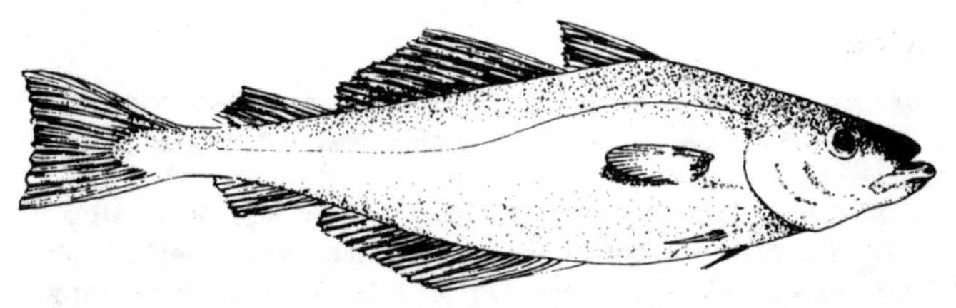

Boat Fishing Methods: (i) Trolling with a plastic sandeel or other suitable lure; (ii) Spinning from a drifting dinghy close in to a reef or rocky headland; (iii) Jigging with a feathered trace; (iv) Deep driftlining with a natural sandeel bait, preferably live.
Baits: Sandeels, peeler crab, mackerel strip. Ragworm are also good for the smaller inshore pollack.

SHARK

Four species of shark are taken on rod and line in British waters – the Blue Shark, the Porbeagle, the Mako and the Thresher Shark. Of these the Blue Shark is the most common, and it is the one most likely to be caught by the newcomer to shark fishing.
Season: Summer and early autumn.
Habitat: Nomadic. Normally encountered several miles offshore, but in warm anticyclonic weather blue shark, porbeagles and (to a lesser degree) threshers may venture quite close inshore.

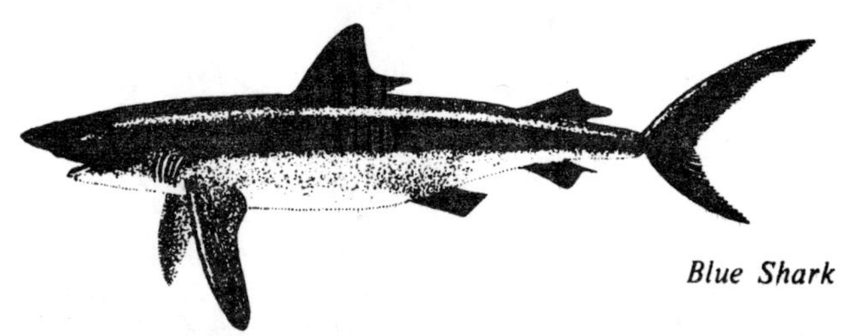

Blue Shark

Fishing Methods: Shark fishing is nearly always carried on from a sizeable professionally skippered boat. The shark are attracted to the drifting boat by laying down a 'rubby-dubby' (groundbait) trail. The size and power of the fish makes it essential to use a suitable rod and reel – the most important item being the reel, which should be of the multiplier type and possess an adequate line capacity. The actual strength of the tackle depends very much on the skill of the angler, and on whether the area being fished is likely to yield only modest-sized blues, or possibly a giant porbeagle or mako.

In either case, shark fishing calls for specialist methods, and space limitations prevent us from going into lengthy details here. The beginner would be well advised to visit one of the recognized shark fishing centres – most of which are are situated around the coasts of Devon and Cornwall. Most skippers of sharking boats hire out suitable tackle, and will provide instruction in its use.

Bait: A whole mackerel is the most common sharking bait, but porbeagle shark will also go for a small whole pollack or coalfish.

THORNBACK RAY

Coloration: This comparatively small member of the skate tribe is usually a blotchy mixture of grey, browns and black on the upper side; white underneath. It is armed with numerous sharp thornlike spines on the wings and tail.

Season: Taken all the year round by boat anglers; from about April to December by shore anglers.

Habitat: Lives on the bottom in areas of sand, sandy-mud and shell-grit, especially in the vicinity of scattered rocks.

Shore Fishing Methods: Casting out leger tackle from a steeply shelving beach, pier or suitable rock position.

Boat Fishing Methods: Legering from an anchored boat, using a flowing trace and a size 3/0 or 4/0 hook. Rays are also taken over clean ground by drift-fishing.

Baits: Mackerel and herring strips; sandeels (fresh or frozen).

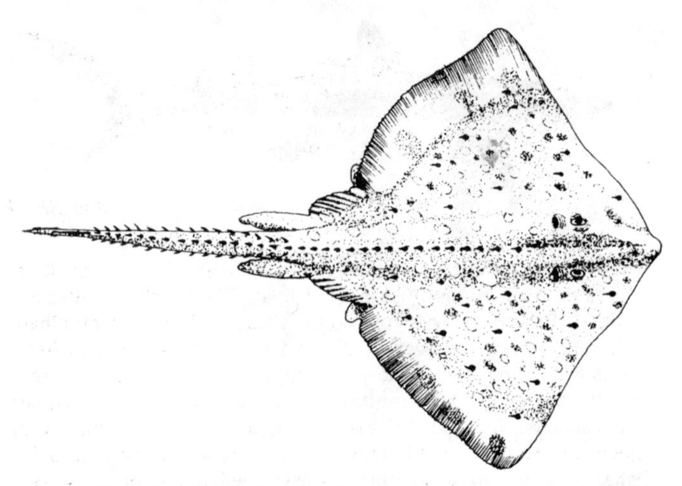

NOTE: Various other species of rays are likely to be taken in addition to the very common Thornback. These include the Small-eyed Ray, Homelyn Ray, Blonde Ray, Sandy Ray, Cuckoo Ray, Sting Ray and Undulate Ray. All are caught on similar tackle and baits, but most (with the exception of the Small-eyed Ray and Sting Ray) are taken almost exclusively by boat anglers.

TOPE

Coloration: This comparatively small member of the shark family is usually dull grey or brownish on the back, becoming white underneath.
Season: Mainly taken by shore and inshore boat anglers during the summer and autumn.
Habitat: Nomadic, roving wherever food is abundant. It feeds on smaller fish, and often ventures close inshore near rocky headlands, reefs and estuary sandbanks.
Shore Fishing: At a few favoured steeply-shelving beaches and rock stations it is possible to catch tope on leger tackle carrying a 4ft plastic-covered wire trace, and forged hook baited with a mackerel fillet or large fresh sandeel. A medium shorecasting rod will prove adequate for tope fishing, and there is no need for the line to be heavier than 25lb breaking strain – provided there is plenty of it, and a 20ft, 35lb b.s. shock leader is knotted to the end of the line to absorb the initial strain of casting.
Boat Fishing: Legering with a sliding lead 'stopped' with a piece of matchstick or valve rubber about 20ft above the trace. This 'stop' should be strong enough to hold the lead in position

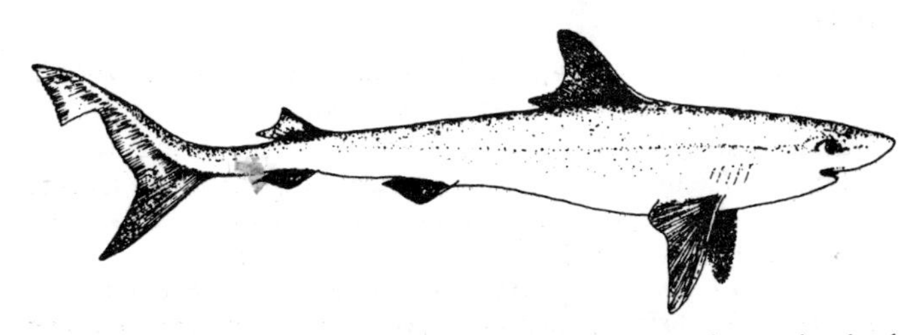

during normal fishing, but weak enough to release the lead when it presses against the end ring of the rod on reeling in.

The trace should be of flexible cable-laid stainless steel wire, about 7ft long and swivelled at either end. The hook (to wire) is best attached to the trace with a spiral locking connector, so that a new hook and wire snood can be attached to the trace without unnecessary delay after boating a tope.

NOTE: In the interests of conservation, tope should be returned unharmed to the water as quickly as possible after capture. For this reason they should not be gaffed, but lifted aboard by grasping them with one hand around the 'wrist' of the tail, and with the other hand on the dorsal fin.

TURBOT

Coloration: This highly prized flatfish is usually brownish or greyish on the upper side, mottled and speckled with numerous lighter and darker markings. The underside is white.

Season: From about May to October over inshore marks.

Habitat: Often found on the edge of steep-to submerged banks of shell-grit or fine sand – particularly in areas where tides run fast.

Fishing Methods: A few turbot are caught from steeply shelving beaches, but they are taken by chance while bottom fishing for other species. For specialist turbot fishing, therefore, one must go afloat, and terminal tackle consists of a leger rig with flowing nylon trace, fished either at anchor or on the drift. The choice of method will depend mainly on the strength of the local tides. Where tides (and drift) are very fast, it is necessary to use an anchor. The tackle must then be fairly powerful, because turbot attain quite a large size, and although they don't put up much of a fight, they do offer quite a lot of water resistance in a fast run of tide.

Baits: Favourite bait is a fillet cut from the side of a greater sandeel, but a fillet of mackerel cut to look like a sandeel is also good.

WHITING

Coloration: Bronzy-brown above, shading to silvery underneath. The lateral line is a thin, brownish seam.

Season: Large shoals of whiting come inshore during late autumn and remain until about February, depending on locality and the weather. Deepwater marks yield whiting over a more extended period, including summer in some areas.

Habitat: Whiting shoals feed mainly close to the bottom on smaller fish, shrimps, etc. They favour areas of fine sand and shell-grit.

Shore Fishing Methods: In late autumn and winter it is possible to take good catches of whiting by casting out a light nylon leger or paternoster from a suitable pier or steeply shelving beach.

Boat Fishing: Deep-sea in summer; inshore in winter. (i) Boomed paternoster, usually fished a foot or two above the bottom. This method can be used either from a drifting or anchored boat. (ii) Driftlining from an anchored boat.

Baits: Lugworm, ragworm, mussels; small strips of herring, mackerel or other whiting; sprats.

WRASSE

Although several species of wrasse inhabit British waters, the only two of worthwhile size are the Ballan Wrasse and the Cuckoo Wrasse.

Cuckoo Wrasse are very colourful, with the males flaunting themselves in vivid hues of red, orangy-yellow and fluorescent blue. The female is predominantly reddish, with black blotches and spots. They are mostly taken by boat anglers.

The Ballan Wrasse is the largest species, and is frequently taken from rocky shore positions. It provides interesting sport on reasonably light tackle. Its coloration is very variable, and often includes background shades of brown or greenish-brown, with flecks and net-like markings of orangy-red, greens, blues and purple.

Season: Summer and autumn.

Shore Fishing: (i) Light single-hook nylon paternoster cast out on to the bottom close alongside a rocky vantage point. In snaggy areas it is wise to attach the lead by a short length of nylon which has a lower breaking strain than the trace and reel line. This method usually catches the biggest fish. (ii) Sliding float tackle fished close to kelpy rocks.

Boat Fishing: Driftlining or paternostering at anchor over rocky ground.

Baits: Small hardbacked crabs, prawns, ragworm, lugworm, cockle, mussel, limpet are all attractive to Ballan Wrasse. In addition, Cuckoo Wrasse will take small strips of mackerel.

Mudeford (See Chart 1)

(With Highcliffe and Christchurch Harbour)

TIDES Double HW: – 3h 14m HW London Bridge. Rise: About 5ft on the bar. Depths: On the bar – about 1½ ft at LW Springs, and 7ft at HW. In the Christchurch Channel – depths vary between 3 – 10ft.

There is a bottleneck at the entrance to Christchurch Harbour, between the Mudeford shore and a spit of sand and shingle. Through these narrows the tide flows very fast, and on the ebb it is said to attain a speed of nearly 9 knots at times during freshets. The length of the spit is always altering, and when entering or leaving harbour, boat anglers should follow carefully the channel marked by buoys.

TOPOGRAPHY Mudeford is a popular centre for sea anglers and boating enthusiasts, situated at the mouth of Christchurch Harbour. This natural harbour is a broad and almost landlocked estuary, which mostly dries out on the E side at LW. A buoyed channel negotiable by small craft leads around the S side of the harbour to the Town Quay at Christchurch.

It is possible to launch a car-trailed dinghy at Mudeford, Stanpit or Christchurch. Mudeford is recommended, as it offers good parking and other facilities.

The shoreline from Milford-on-Sea to Highcliffe is popular with family holiday anglers, as there is safe swimming by day, and good shore fishing towards evening. The shore at Highcliffe is sandy.

SHORE FISHING

1 Beckton Bunny A comparatively quiet stretch of beach underneath the cliff-top Golf Course. Produces bass, rays, flatfish (including some big sole); also occasional sting-ray and monkfish.

2 Barton Fishing can be good, especially in the evening and at night. Some large bass at times; also rays, conger and flatfish.

3 Chewton Bunny A popular fishing spot. Two-hook Wessex leger recommended, with 'double-interest' baits. Catches include thornback rays (mainly after dark), bass (rough sea improves daylight prospects), flounders and sole. Baits: razorfish (good for rays and bass), herring and mackerel cuttings, slipper limpet, ragworm and sandeels (fresh or frozen).

4 Highcliffe Beach often crowded in summer by day, but night fishing yields bass and rays on razorfish, squid and cuttings of herring or mackerel. Also occasional sole or ragworm, etc., after dark. Best months for bass here are April and May, and September and October for the larger ones. Occasional winter codling in some years.

5 Mudeford Wall Known locally as 'Slippery Slopes', owing to the seaweed covering lower part. The outer side, bordering the harbour entrance, is a likely place for bass and flounders. They are taken on sandeels, slipper limpet, peeler crab, bunched ragworms, herring and lugworm. Both ground and float tackle are used – crabs, seaweed, boat traffic and the very strong tides permitting! By day sport is usually slow, and it is much better to try in the very early morning, late evening, and during slack tide. Spinning for bass is also possible.

6 Tide Run, South Side Just across the harbour entrance, facing Mudeford, is a long spit of sand and shingle. Casting out from here into the tide-run with light leger tackle baited with fresh sandeel sometimes produces bass. Spinning can also be productive, and artificial lures should resemble a sandeel (i.e. plastic sandeel, German sprat, ABU 'Krill', Intrepid 'Flectolite', etc.). Cast up-tide and allow the current to swing the bait down and around while retrieving. The best fishing times are around dawn and towards dusk, early flood and slack HW.

7 Avon Beach This commences just E of Slippery Slopes (Mark 5), where a fine stretch of shingle and sand runs for 200 yards or more to the Avon Beach car park. A very popular shore casting area, yielding mainly bass (some large) and flounders – the latter mostly in winter. Suggest two-hook tackle with double-interest baits.

8 Hengistbury Head Area A stone groyne juts out from the rocky shore of Hengistbury Head. From here it is possible to take bass (some large) and wrasse on sliding float tackle, and conger on patches of clear ground using large fish and squid baits. Some of the conger run to a good size, and while these notes were being compiled one of 29lb was caught by baiting with a small wrasse caught at the same place. Good baits for bass are sandeels, small live pouting and wrasse, razorfish, slipper limpet, squid and ragworm.

When conditions are quiet, grey mullet can sometimes be taken with light quill float tackle or, alternatively, with a tiny

The author unhooks a turbot caught while inshore dinghy fishing with legered mackerel strip off the the Dorset coast.

Large bass often venture close in to this type of rocky shoreline. Here an angler is using light spinning tackle and an artificial lure in the first light of dawn — possibly the most productive time of all for reef bass. Another peak feeding time for bass and pollack is the final hour between sundown and dusk, especially when this period coincides with an incoming tide.

Shore anglers stand silhouetted against the after-glow as dusk falls on Seatown beach. The far end of this beach is dominated by the dark bulk of Golden Cap, highest point on the south coast.

The author captured this 12 lb. 10 oz. bass by drifting a live sandeel from a dinghy just outside the mouth of Poole Harbour. Equally good results can often be obtained by fishing a live prawn close to a tidal reef.

fly-spoon baited with a 1-inch length of harbour ragworm. Deep water (down to 30ft) lies on the W side of the groyne, but it is more shallow on E side (down to about 10ft). Very shallow straight out from groyne, with seaweed-covered rocks.

Fishing on either side of the Head, where the shore adjoins reasonably clean ground, also produces fair mixed fishing – especially after dark. The Hengistbury fishing area can be reached from Mudeford by taking the ferry across the harbour, and then walking; or from Hengistbury Head car park, at the W side. Incidentally, much of the headland area is a nature reserve, with a signposted nature trail.

MULLET FISHING There are opportunities for mullet fishing inside Christchurch Harbour, using various light tackle techniques, ranging from a light quill float rig baited with bread crust or paste to spinning with a tiny fly-spoon baited with a small piece of red harbour rag. Any suitable vantage point, fished early in the morning before boats are on the move, is likely to produce results, but preliminary groundbaiting – preferably over a period of several days – is advisable.

BOAT FISHING

9 Christchurch Harbour Fishing is only permitted at the Mudeford-Hengistbury Head end of the harbour; the limits being defined by notice boards erected alongside the channels. There are comparatively few sizeable bass in the harbour, but often plenty of school bass, and some good flounders. Mullet are also plentiful. The bass fishing is usually best during the flood tide, but the time of day also seems to be important. Try the very early morning and evening. Peeler crab and bunched ragworm are useful baits. These can be legered, but a float prevents crabs robbing the bait.

Flounders can be caught on a light nylon leger, paternoster-trot or baited-spoon along edge of main Christchurch Channel marked by buoys – *but do not obstruct the channel.* One good place is near the yacht moorings; another alongside the second pair of buoys. Bunched ragworm fished during the flood tide produces good results.

10 Christchurch Ledge This narrow ledge of submerged rock extends for about 2¾ miles SE from Hengistbury Head. Fairly close inshore, on the E side of the Head, there is a chance of contacting bass, using the following methods: (i) Trolling slowly and quietly with a live sandeel or 'Red Gill' plastic sandeel. (ii) Drift-trolling in a dinghy with an unweighted or very lightly weighted line baited with a live sandeel or live prawn – the dinghy being allowed to drift with the tide, with an occasional pull on the oars *across the tide* to keep the line streamed astern.

(iii) Float fishing.

Apart from bass (when present), and mackerel trolling, the fishing is not very good on the E side of the Ledge, owing to strong currents and hordes of wrasse. For general fishing the W side is much better, and at several places about 1-2½ miles offshore catches of pollack, pouting, bream, huss, conger, rays, wrasse, tope and lesser spotted dogfish are made by paternostering, driftlining or legering, according to species. A night fishing session for conger can be particularly rewarding, with eels up to 40lb a possibility.

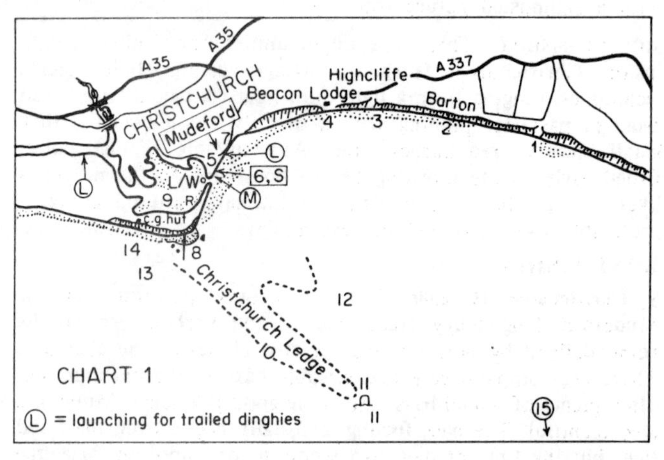

The Ledge can usually be located during the summer months by the lobster pots set along it. Also by taking a line from the cage-beacon at end of Hengistbury Groyne to the Ledge Buoy (visible on bright, clear days) or to a point about 15 deg. S of the Needles, Isle of Wight. When legering for such bottom species as conger, tope and huss, however, it is best to use a plummet or echo-sounder to position the boat accurately over clean ground close alongside a good rocky mark. Baits: herring and mackerel slips (bream, pouting), strips (pollack, conger, rays, huss), fillets (tope, large conger and huss); lugworm (bream, pouting, wrasse); ragworm (pollack, bream, pouting, wrasse); sandeels – driftlined (pollack).

11 Ledge Buoy Area The seaward extremity of Christchurch Ledge is marked by a buoy, and there are several good positions for tope and general ground fishing in this area. One lies about 200 yards on the inshore side of the buoy, towards a conspicuous white house (Beacon Lodge) near Highcliffe. Another lies 150 yards SE of the buoy.

12 Halfway Rock This mark actually lies rather more than halfway between Mudeford and the Ledge Buoy. To locate, steer SE after leaving Christchurch Harbour until the boat is on a line between Beacon Lodge and the Ledge Buoy. Then, with Beacon Lodge under the stern, head towards the Ledge Buoy until Hurst Point just draws clear of Sconce Point on the NW shore of Wight. (Visible on clear days.) Rocks lie fairly close W of this mark, and for best results the angler lacking local knowledge or an echo-sounder should pinpoint them by dragging a weight along the sea-bed, and then fish on clear ground close alongside. This mark yields black bream, conger, huss, pollack, tope, pouting and lesser spotted dogfish. Baits as for Mark 10.

13 Pout Hole This is a useful inshore mark for general all-round fishing. It lies on a line with Beacon Lodge near Highcliffe and the cage-beacon at the end of Hengistbury Groyne, and about halfway between the groyne and the Coastguard Look-out on Hengistbury Head.

This is a very popular mark, yielding variable catches ranging from sole (some large) to tope (up to 30lb or more). It reaches a considerable depth for this inshore area – 10 fathoms LWOS. Baits as for Mark 10.

14 The Look-out Mark Situated about 200 yards straight out from the Coastguard Look-out on Hengistbury Head cliff-edge. A very good sandy patch for plaice, dabs, etc.

15 Dolphin Bank This sandy shoal lies some 6-7 miles offshore from Mudeford. Very strong tides run from here to the Hurst Narrows and Shingles, and a sizeable craft and experienced boatman are essential. It is a good mark for plaice and rays, with the occasional monkfish and sting-ray in season. The N and S fringes of the bank (towards the E end) are often a good area for tope.

Christchurch Bay Besides the marks described above, many less localised species of fish are taken in Christchurch Bay. Mackerel are likely to be encountered almost anywhere during summer months, while thornback rays and dabs are taken within ½-¾ mile of the shore, notably off Chewton Bunny. Sole are also found off Chewton Bunny, usually about 1 mile offshore. Flounders and dabs may be caught close in to the seaward side of the spit at the entrance to Christchurch Harbour. Other spots are likely to yield tope, monkfish, plaice and the occasional turbot – although the latter have become rather scarce in recent years.

Boat Hire

Deep-sea fishing trips can be arranged with local boatmen

working out of Mudeford. For up-to-date information consult any of the tackle dealers listed below.

Tackle and Bait Dealers
Pro Fishing Tackle, 258 Barrack Road, Christchurch. Tel: 484518.
Davis Fishing Tackle, 75 Bargate, Christchurch. Tel: 485169.
Christchurch Angling Centre, 7 Castle Parade, Iford Bridge, Christchurch. Tel: 480520.

Local Bait Grounds (Chart Symbols are shown in brackets)
Lugworms (L/W) can be dug on various sandflats in Christchurch Harbour, notably the one opposite the entrance. Be sure to anchor the dinghy when landing on this flat at LW – the water rises very quickly here when the tide turns.

Ragworms (R). Small harbour ragworms can be dug at selected places, notably on shores where there is a mixture of sand and mud.

Sandeels (S) may be found at times on the sandy spit which runs out on the seaward side of the harbour entrance. They are obtained by digging or scratching in the sand *close to the water's edge.* Best results usually at low Springs, though they may be found during less favourable tides.

Peeler Crabs (C) are not very plentiful, but may sometimes be found in old tin cans lying in the harbour mud, or by probing with a crab-hook along the base of quay walls, etc.

Mussels (M). Large mussels are plentiful on the quay wall at Mudeford, but are so coated with weedy growths that they can be easily overlooked. They are most easily reached from a dinghy at slack LW Springs.

Local Sea Angling Club
Christchurch and District Fishing Club,

Bournemouth Area (See also Chart 2)

(With Southbourne and Boscombe)

TIDES Double HW: – 3h 23m (approx.) London Bridge. Rise: 6½ ft at Springs; 4¾ ft at Neaps. Tidal Streams: Within a mile or so of the Bournemouth-Southbourne shore the tidal streams are weak, but very strong tides flow in and out of Poole Harbour entrance.

TOPOGRAPHY The towns of Bournemouth, Boscombe and Southbourne adjoin each other along a 5 mile stretch of coast. For much of this distance the shoreline consists of gently shelving sand, and there is a fair run of surf when the wind blows strongly between SE and SW. At times when fishing from these sands it is an advantage to be able to cast out a good distance, and thigh waders are useful. The beach becomes very crowded with swimmers during the holiday season, and then shore-casting is only possible at night.

There is no parking on the promenades except the Undercliff Drive, which is open by day from October to mid-May, with a closure over the Easter period.

There was a time when the shore and boat fishing at Bournemouth was very productive, but catches have dwindled considerably in recent years. However, first-class sport is often obtainable nearby at Poole Harbour and Sandbanks, and towards Hengistbury Head.

SHORE FISHING

During the peak holiday months daytime fishing is not recommended on the main pleasure beaches, due to the large numbers of swimmers. Night fishing, however, is always worth a trial. Sea conditions normally permit the use of reasonably light tackle, and recommended terminal traces include the Wessex leger, single-hook leger and running paternoster.

Hengistbury Head Area There is good general shore fishing from the shingle beach, and catches include some decent-sized bass, flatfish and (at night) conger from the E end. This area often fishes particularly well in the autumn, and in some years winter cod may also be encountered.

1 Southbourne Beach The Solent Road area, at extreme E end of Southbourne, is a useful shore-casting spot for flounders, plaice, dabs and at night occasional sole on legered ragworm. There is a car park at Solent Road. The Southbourne Promenade area, after dark, is also capable of yielding bass when a moderate surf is running. Use light nylon paternoster or leger tackle. Good general purpose baits are ragworm, lugworm, slipper limpet and razorfish.

2 Boscombe Beach Similar to Mark 1. The shoreline under the Promenade yields bass, plaice and dabs; also whiting in late autumn and winter.

3 Boscombe Pier Fishing is allowed from October to March during the hours the pier is open to the public. Dependent on weather conditions, this is usually from 9 am to 5 pm. This pier stands in a rewarding spot for plaice, soles, flounders and bass. Baits: ragworm, lugworm, razorfish, slipper limpet. For flatfish, try a combination of float and baited-spoon.

4 Bournemouth Pier Fishing is allowed on the lower landing stage only during the period the pier is open to the public. Dependent on weather conditions, this is usually from 9 am to 5 pm or 6 pm. The inclusive charge is quite reasonable. Bass are taken, but catches have fallen off in recent years. Other species include dabs and occasional plaice. Flounders are sometimes present in winter when these fish are working out into the open sea for spawning. Baits: ragworm, razorfish, slipper limpet. Whiting often put in an appearance in late autumn and winter. Baits, lug, herring strips, etc. Mullet are caught in suitable summer conditions, using fine tackle and a size 10 hook baited with small harbour ragworms or bread (paste, crust or flake).

5 Durley Chine Shore casting with tackle and baits similar to Mark 1. Some bass are caught mainly after dark. Plaice, too, are sometimes present in numbers, particularly in late summer and early autumn. Durley Rocks (submerged) lie a short distance offshore here, and after-dark distance casting with suitable baits may yield pouting or the occasional conger.

6 Flaghead Chine to Sandbanks Good quality flounders during the winter months on legered ragworm. Also large bass at times – mainly after dark from about late May to early November. Recommended baits: razorfish, sandeel (preferably fresh) and slipper limpet.

BOAT FISHING

7 Southbourne About ¾ mile off Southbourne there are a number of useful fishing spots for plaice and dabs, and these extend E a little way towards Hengistbury Head. Suggested method: light nylon leger or paternoster-trot, with ragworm or lug baits on fine-wire hooks.

8 Boscombe Pier A useful area for inshore boat fishing lies a short distance off this pier. Catches consist mainly of plaice and dabs, using tackle and baits suggested under Mark 7. Bass by trolling – sometimes. Whiting in late autumn and winter, using paternoster or single-hook flowing trace, fished deep.

9 Durley Rock Plaice are sometimes caught on sandy ground surrounding this submerged rock – especially in late summer. It lies about ¼ mile offshore and ½ mile W of Bournemouth Pier. A light leger or two-hook paternoster-trot baited with lug

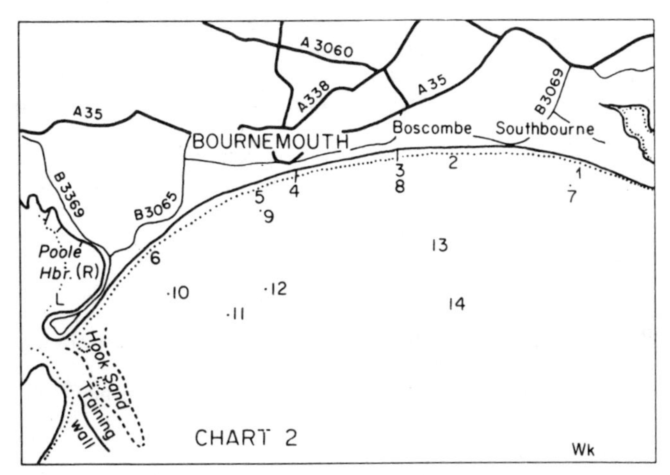

or ragworm is a useful method. Also, anglers with local knowledge take large bags by drifting along the edge of rough ground from Woodbury Rock (10), past Bournemouth Rocks, to Durley Rocks. Bass are occasionally taken by trolling in the area. Driftlining at anchor accounts for black bream in season, as well as pouting. Legering with heavier gear yields conger, dogfish and the occasional medium-sized turbot.

10, 11 and 12 Poole Rocks There are several rocky marks in the bay off Bournemouth, but they are most conveniently fished by boats working out of Poole Harbour. The following are three rewarding positions: Woodbury Rock, or Inner Poole Patch (10) – situated directly off Flaghead Chine about $\frac{3}{4}$ mile offshore; Middle Poole Patch, otherwise known as Lobster Rock (11), about 1$\frac{3}{4}$ miles off Canford Cliffs, and Outer Poole Patch (12) about 1 mile ENE from Mark 11.

Owing to the very built-up nature of the nearby coast it is difficult to give cross-bearings for locating these places, but much of the intervening sea-bed is a mixture of sand and scattered rock, and yields rays, black bream, conger, dogfish, pouting, plaice, occasional tope, etc.

Mackerel, scad and garfish are likely to be encountered anywhere in the bay during summer months; while on suitable ground some good flatfish, including sole, are taken with light leger or paternoster-trot tackle baited with razorfish, lug or ragworm.

13 and 14 Boscombe Rough This is a fairly large area of shingle and small rocks about 1$\frac{3}{4}$ miles SSW from the end of Boscombe Pier. Offers good ground fishing for tope, rays, black bream and conger during summer; also cod and whiting from about November to early February. Gurnard are not unusual. Baits: herring, squid, sprats, razorfish. There is also the Outer Rough (14), approximately ¾ mile further out. Similar baits and tackle.

These fishing grounds lie near the edge of the strong tidal streams flowing between Handfast Point and Hengistbury Head – hence the good fishing.

Tackle and Bait Dealers

Multi-Sports, 225 Old Christchurch Road, Bournemouth. Tel: 556319.

Bournemouth Fishing Lodge (Ivor Brittain), 904 Wimborne Road, Moordown, Bournemouth. Tel: 514345.

G. Courage, 131-133 Seabourne Rd., Southbourne, Bournemouth. Tel: 432971.

Local Bait Grounds

See under **Poole Harbour.**

Local Sea Angling Clubs

Bournemouth and District S.A.A.
Boscombe and Southbourne S.F.C.
Bay Angling Society
Poole Dolphins S.A.C.

(Up-to-date details from most local tackle dealers)

Poole Harbour Area (See also Chart 3)

TIDES The coast here is visited by two separate tidal 'waves', resulting in Double High Water. Tidal predictions are complicated by the fact that the interval between the high waters is greater inside the harbour than at the entrance, as well as being subject to certain other variations. At the entrance the times of high water are approximately: –5h 00m and –1h 30m HW London Bridge. Rise: 6½ ft at Springs; 4¾ ft at Neaps.

Reference to the accompanying chart will show that a bottle-neck exists between the Sandbanks promontory and South Haven Point, and through this a considerable tide flows on the ebb and flood. The flood begins –4h 30m 1st HW Poole, and attains at Springs a rate of 2½ – 3 knots. The ebb begins + 0h 15m 1st HW Poole, flowing weakly for approximately the first 2½ hours; then attaining a rate of 4 – 5 knots.

TOPOGRAPHY Poole Harbour is a vast tidal lake, with a creek-indented shoreline approximately 100 miles in length. The busy commercial port of Poole is situated on the N shore, but the borough boundaries also embrace the beautiful suburbs of Sandbanks, Canford Cliffs and Branksome Park. The latter are situated close to the open sea, and possess a pleasant stretch of shore.

There is good and varied fishing all round the Harbour, and also out to sea. Anglers and boat-minded families who like to avoid the crowds can have endless fun fishing and exploring the lonely channels of the W and S shores. Here the waters are fringed by wild heathlands – the vast and rather forbidding 'Egdon Heath' of the Hardy novels.

A word of warning is necessary, however. Poole Harbour's 10,000 acres of water can become really choppy in windy weather, also numerous weed and mud-banks are exposed at low tide, and great care must be taken not to go aground. Most of the 'lakes', and many of the beaches, dry out very quickly after the second high water because they are so flat. Thick mud extends for much farther than one could push a boat, and in many places, owing to the thousands of springs in the ground, it would be really dangerous to attempt to do so – the mud being almost bottomless in places.

So, before you go exploring, be sure you know your tides; don't stray far from the main channels, and if by chance you *do* get stuck on a mud-bank, STAY IN THE BOAT.

SHORE FISHING

A very wide choice of fishing stations is available to the shore angler around Poole Harbour, and it is only possible to mention here a few of the more popular places. The fish most commonly found inside the harbour are bass, flounders, plaice and mullet, but other species, such as mackerel, scad, etc. are seasonal visitors.

The flatfish, in particular, tend to move from mark to mark, mainly due to seasonal influences. A visiting angler is therefore advised to make enquiries locally on arrival as to which fishing positions are yielding best results at the moment. Flounders are mostly caught with bottom tackle, as described under Mark 2 below, but where bait-robbing crabs make themselves a nuisance it often helps to use a 'buoyant leger' trace incorporating a small balsa float a few inches in front of the hook. This 'crab-beater' tackle lifts the baited hook just out of reach of crabs, and actually seems to make the bait more attractive to flatfish. When conditions are suitable, however, the baited-spoon method is also capable of providing good results.

1 Poole Quay A convenient fishing spot close to the town. Daytime fishing yields some flounders, but night fishing is best, and at times yields reasonably good bass – particularly near the bridge. Ragworm is a popular bait, but live prawns are also worth trying. Tiny pollack can also be caught close in under the wall, and these likewise make a good livebait for the bass. Mullet can be taken on light quill float tackle and bread baits by those prepared to fish very early in the morning.

2 Hamworthy Try a light nylon monofil paternoster, leger or paternoster-trot, with ragworm bait. Flounders are present in fair numbers, and in the autumn a few sole are taken here. The latter are often of quite good size. Mullet may also be present when conditions are quiet, and are sometimes taken on light quill float tackle.

3 Salterns Pier Bass on float tackle or by spinning. Flounders with a leger or paternoster-trot.

4 and 5 Sandbanks This is the name given to the township on the spit of land which juts out to form the N arm of Poole Harbour entrance. It is a good area for bass, and there are several places suitable for shore fishing. One good spot is the stretch of sandy shore overlooking the Main Channel, nearly opposite the castle on Brownsea Island (4). One convenient feature of this mark is that bait can be dug on the spot around low tide. Leger tackle, or a running paternoster, yields good results. When casting out, care must be taken to avoid boat moorings, which are numerous along this stretch of shore. Ragworm bait is popular, and this will also take flounders.

The Sandbanks area is particularly good for flounders around January, when these fish are heading out towards their spawning grounds in the open sea. A good time to try for them is just before low water, casting well out towards the channel.

Late night fishing for bass can also be good near the ferry (5). There is a patch of sandy shore just NW of the ferry slip, near a stranded wreck. By day this is used by the motor boat ferries, but at night, after these have stopped running, try casting out leger tackle baited generously with squid. King ragworm, sandeel and razorfish are some other good baits. The tide flows hard here, and a pyramid-shaped leger lead is recommended, rather than a barrel lead which is likely to roll in the current.

Spinning is a rewarding daytime method for bass when conditions are suitable, using either natural sandeel baits or artificials such as the 'Red Gill' plastic sandeel, rubber eels, German sprat and medium-sized wobbling spoons.

6 South Haven Point This is the promontory which forms the

S shore of Poole Harbour entrance. The sandy shore just seaward of the ferry slip is a good bass fishing spot. Methods similar to Marks 4 and 5.

7 Shell Bay A favourite picnic spot, and towards the SE end of the beach there is a fair chance of catching bass and flatfish by the methods described under Marks 4 and 5. The first of the flood is a good time to start fishing, and a likely place to cast out is near some scattered rocks marking the end of a stone groyne or breakwater. Night fishing is best for bass, but don't miss the last ferry back to Poole!

Baits: king ragworm, razorfish, slipper limpet, frozen herring, sandeel.

8 Poole Bay A number of useful places for shore fishing are to be found along the shores of Poole Bay. Bass and flounders are taken here, also occasional plaice. Ragworm bait, which is so popular in Poole Harbour, is also productive here. In addition, it is worth trying slipper limpet, razorfish and sandeels. Night fishing brings best results with the bass.

BOAT FISHING

NOTE: Restrictions in Poole Harbour. (i) It is forbidden to obstruct with boat or tackle any channel used by vessels; nor must one drift in a fairway for the purpose of fishing. (ii) **Bass Nursery Area.** From 1 May to 31 October it is forbidden to boat fish for bass within a line drawn from Jerry's Point to Saltern's Pier, and passing through Branksea Castle on Brownsea Island. Please keep these bye-laws in mind when reading the following notes.

9 Holes Bay Good for flounders. Best tackle: light nylon paternoster, baited-spoon, or combination of float and baited-spoon. Baits: rag or razorfish. Lug is no good here. Some good bass caught by Hamworthy Bridge, usually from May onwards.

10 Wareham Channel A useful area for flounders and occasional plaice. Methods as for Mark 9. Try also the S side of Wareham Channel entrance on an ebbing spring tide.

11 Middle Ground Drifting for flounders and plaice, using the tackles described under Mark 9. Middle Ground is a drying bank which divides the main channel to Poole, and it is marked by can-shaped buoys bearing the words: 'S Middle Ground' and 'E Middle Ground'. The deepest water is on the E and N sides of the bank, and anglers should bear in mind that this is the channel used by large vessels. One useful drifting area lies just

W of the area that dries at LW Springs. An alternative spot is near the Aunt Betty Buoy (No. 54) a short distance to the S. A good time to fish here is towards HW or around half-ebb. Given a suitable wind, try drifting between the buoy and the stakes, as this area has an attraction for plaice up to 4lb or more.

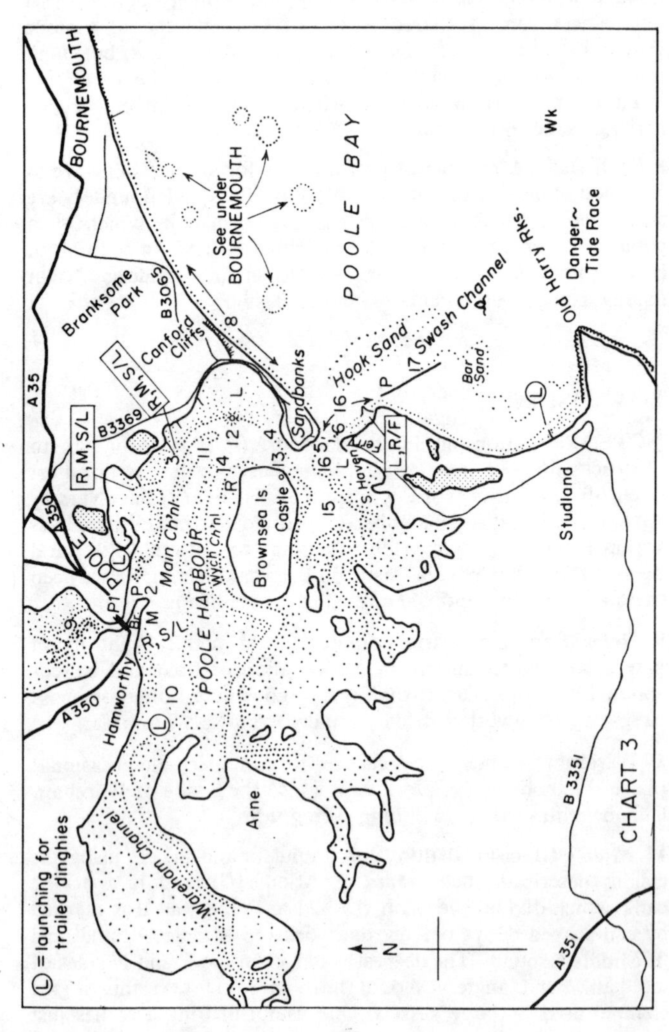

12 Bulpitt Light This light is situated on a black iron framework beacon about ¾ mile N of Sandbanks. Anchor on edge of channel and fish towards the beacon. Good catches of flounders and occasional plaice are sometimes taken in this area, using a ragworm-baited buoyant leger or float-fished spoon. The bottom is rough.

13 Brownsea Castle There is deep water a little way off the shore of Brownsea Island, near Brownsea Castle. Catches include bass, plaice, flounders and dabs; also pouting and a few conger where the bottom is extra rocky. The plaice can be taken at anchor, the peak periods being around HW and half-ebb. The bass can be fished for on the drift with a sandeel. This is best done around HW, when the tide-run eases off.

14 Wych Channel Entrance Large plaice sometimes found here, particularly in May or June. Fish about 100 yards or more from stakes area for the biggest fish. Drifting possible in about 2 fathoms.

15 South Deep There are two main alternatives in this area: (i) Fishing at anchor near the can stake for flounders and occasional plaice. An ebbing spring tide usually gives best results. School bass also present sometimes. All the usual baits work here, and slipper limpet (plentiful in this area) are also killing. Anchor on edge of channel and fish into deeper water. (ii) Drifting with wind and tide along the edge of the channel. Catches include plaice, flounders and dabs.

NOTE: In all parts of the South Deep area the best results are generally obtained near channel edges, particularly when tides are running hard.

16 Haven Entrance An excellent bass fishing area because all fish entering or leaving Poole Harbour are bound to pass through these narrows. Favourite method is drifting with the tide, with a live sandeel or small pouting presented on a light flowing trace. Local boatmen who specialise in taking out parties of anglers for this type of fishing use a sandeel seine to obtain supplies of fresh bait. *This is the secret of their success,* and the private boat angler fishing without suitable livebait is unlikely to do so well.

Owing to the strong tides, it is necessary to use a motor in order to recover lost ground between drifts.

There are three main drift areas: (i) To seaward of the ferry route, close in to the Haven Hotel edge of the Swash Channel, and extending as far as the first buoy in the channel; (ii) Inside the ferry route on the Sandbanks side; (iii) Inside the ferry route near Stoney Island – drifting between the red and white buoys.

The outer buoy area is reputed to be most productive on the ebb, and the inner buoy area on the flood.

17 Training Wall and Swash Channel This is really a continuation of the fishing area just described under Mark 15. From the SE end of Shell Bay a stone training wall extends out to sea for about ¾ mile, and bass are often present in its vicinity. They can be taken with a variety of trolling baits – two worth trying are fresh sandeel, or a 'Red Gill' plastic sandeel. After passing the beacon marking the end of the training wall, bear away to the S for ½ mile, trolling round the edge of the Bar Sand.

Driftlining for bass with live prawns close in to the training wall is also rewarding, especially in the evening. Tope are sometimes encountered a little way off the seaward end of the training wall.

WARNING: The training wall is covered between half tide and high water, and should be approached with caution.

Boat Hire

Fishing trips can be arranged through local tackle shops, or with individual boatmen.

Tackle and Bait Dealers

Poole Angling Centre, 19 High Street, Poole. Tel: 674409.
Southern Angling Supplies, 5 High Street, Poole. Tel: 676597.
Dick's Fishing Tackle, 66a High Street, Poole. Tel: 679622.
Wessex Angling Centre, 321 Wimborne Road, Poole. Tel: 668244.

Local Baits

(Chart symbols are shown in brackets)

Ragworms (R) of varying size can be dug on most shores of Poole Harbour where the ground is firm – i.e. not thick mud. Brownsea Island is probably the best place for king ragworm, but the island is strictly private and one has to be very careful not to trespass above high water mark. Smaller ragworm are found in the Poole area, but many of the grounds nearest the town are over-dug. Other areas for medium-sized rag include Goathorn, Redhorn, Newton Point, Lilliput, Baiter's Point and Hamworthy.

NOTE: Anglers are requested to fill in any holes they may have dug before leaving the bait ground. The writer knows of one case at Poole where a small child would have been drowned in one of these holes, had not the mother dashed fully clothed into the sea.

Lugworms (L) are often found in ragworm areas (q.v.), but are more especially found on the W side of Sandbanks (Stokes Bay to Evening Hill). On the South Haven shore, lugworm are plentiful around Shell Bay.

Razorfish (R/F) can be dug on the Shell Bay, Hook Sands and Studland Bay shores for a limited period during low spring tides.

Slipper Limpets (S/L) seem to be fairly widespread, and are most likely to be found at low Springs.

Mussels (M) are found inside the harbour, clustered on piles, quay walls, etc. The largest ones are obtainable at low Springs.

Prawns (P) can be caught with baited drop-nets, known locally as hoop-nets. Kipper is a first-class bait; the oil seems to attract the prawns ... and you can always eat your bait afterwards if you don't catch any prawns!

Hamworthy New Quay, and Poole Quay (near the bridge) are both likely spots. The best catches of all, however, are usually made by working drop-nets from a dinghy near the training wall (See Mark 16). The best time is dusk, or when the water is cloudy.

Local fishermen set prawn pots, which are like very small lobster pots.

Local Sea Angling Clubs
Poole Dolphins S.A.C.

Studland (See also Chart 3)

This picturesque village lies beside a shallow sandy bay. Well sheltered from the W and S it is a convenient place to launch a light, car-trailed dinghy.

Shore fishing is rather poor inside Studland Bay, but there are quite good prospects for bass at South Haven Point and near the E end of Shell Bay, about 3 miles distant. (See under **Poole**

Harbour Area. Marks 6 and 7.)
Boat fishing for bass is good at times, mainly around the Bar Sand and along the E side of the training wall. (See under **Poole Harbour Area,** Mark 17.)

Over the Studland Bay banks, leger tackle baited with razorfish has taken good catches of flounders, plaice, as well as the occasional bass. Lugworm bait, however, gives only poor results.

Some good tope have been taken in the Studland area, including a record-breaking 65-pounder. One likely area is off Handfast Point; another lies a little way off the end of the training wall.

Close in to Old Harry Rocks there is also some boat fishing for smallish pollack, mackerel, occasional bass, conger and dogfish, but watch out for drying rocks. Rays are taken off the headland.

WARNING: A tide race appears off Handfast Point during down-Channel tides, and visiting anglers should only fish this area in *calm* weather, when the tide is flowing up-Channel.

Swanage (See also Chart 4)

TIDES Double High Water similar to Poole Harbour entrance. Rise: 6¼ ft at Springs; 4¼ ft at Neaps. Tidal Streams: Fairly weak inside the bay, but further offshore the down-Channel tide attains a rate of 3 knots, and the up-Channel tide a rate of 1½ knots. There are also tide races off Peveril Point, Handfast Point and St. Alban's Head. At Peveril and Handfast Points the water is most disturbed when the tide is flowing down-Channel.

TOPOGRAPHY Swanage is a fair-sized holiday resort, set in a bay of considerable scenic attractions. There is safe swimming and a long stretch of clean sand ending in chalk cliffs towards Ballard Point. The bay faces E, so inshore fishing marks are sheltered from the prevailing W and SW winds. The motorist-angler trailing his own dinghy will have no difficulty in getting afloat, except during fresh E winds.

Shore

1 Swanage Pier This pier offers rather mediocre fishing, with catches consisting largely of small pouting – although on occasions bass are taken. Bream are also caught in summer from June onwards, some of which are of quite good size (1 ½–2lb). The best fishing is in the evening, when the water is a little cloudy, and under similar conditions small pollack are taken. Small bait-robbing wrasse can be a nuisance on occasions.

Sliding float tackle is used here quite a lot, with ragworm a popular bait. Some local bass anglers prefer to use live prawns.

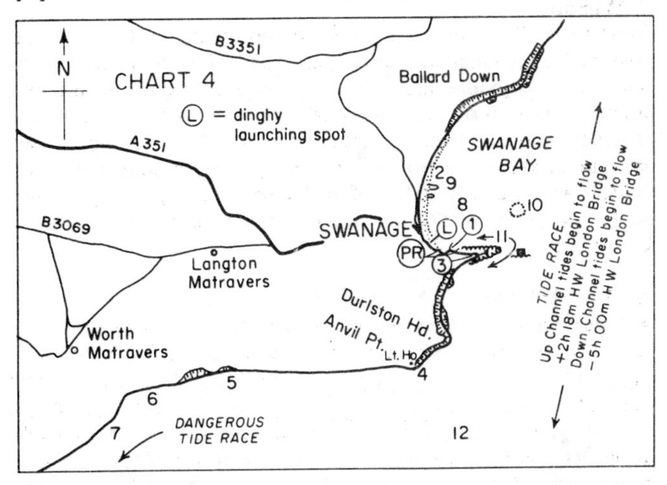

2 Grand Hotel Along the shores of Swanage Bay there is little worthwhile fishing to be had, except in the neighbourhood of the Grand Hotel. Here quite a few good bass have been taken by night anglers using herring strip and large ragworm baits. Some locals contend that better fishing is to be had nearer Ballard Down or towards the end of the beach, where rays of moderate weight are often taken. The sea-bed in this direction becomes progressively more snaggy, however, and to avoid losing tackle it is advisable to use a spoon-shaped lead and a fast-retrieve reel. Incidentally, skin divers have proved that there are plenty of bass off the rocks towards Ballard Point, but this is a difficult area to fish from the shore with rod and line.

3 Peveril Ledge This promontory offers possibilities for rock fishing. Pollack, wrasse and occasional bass are encountered here, and in summer tope sometimes venture close in.

One angler fishing from the end of the ledge during a low Spring tide happened to put his rod down for a moment; then suddenly saw it sliding over the edge of the rocks. He just managed to grab it – only to go over the edge himself. While still sinking into the 'murky depths' he tightened on the fish and struck hard, but the line parted almost immediately. However, another angler fishing nearby saw the fish swirl to the surface, and recognized it as a large tope.

4 Anvil Point Lighthouse
5 Dancing Ledge
6 Seacombe
7 Winspit
Marks 4 to 7 are float fishing spots, producing pollack, wrasse, bass and occasional mackerel. Baits: pollack (ragworm, prawns and – not so good – mackerel strip); wrasse (ragworm, prawns, limpet); bass (prawns, mackerel strip, ragworm); mackerel (mackerel strip). Also in certain places, it is possible to cast ground tackle on to reasonably clear patches among the rocks. Baited with large cuttings of mackerel, herring or squid, this stands a good chance of taking conger, particularly in the evening.

BOAT FISHING

8 Ledge Buoy A short distance out in Swanage Bay there is a patch of weedy rocks marked by a yellow buoy. This is a popular mark with holiday anglers, as it can be reached easily and safely in a hired rowing boat. Plenty of bream are caught here in summer – those of 1½lb being considered reasonably good fish, while quite a few top 2lb. The best bream are usually found 300 yards to seaward of the buoy, with the buoy aligned with the clock tower in the middle of the sea front. Driftline tackle fished fairly deep, and a fairly light rod, are recommended for this species. Baits: ragworm, prawn, lugworm, mackerel strip, mussel.

Other species which may be expected are pollack, pouting and wrasse; and if fish baits are legered on the bottom there is also a chance of taking rays, modest-sized conger, huss and – on the outer fringes of the mark – lesser spotted dogfish.

Mackerel may be encountered anywhere in the bay during the summer months.

9 North Ledge This is a long ledge extending off the Grand Hotel, and it is a useful mark for the dinghy angler. It runs about 200 yards from the beach for approximately ½ mile, and during the summer months its position is usually indicated by the presence of lobster pot corks.

Plenty of black bream are taken here in season, but slack water is a poor time to try for them. Worthwhile results can only be obtained when a tide is running – the direction of the tide does not matter. It should be noted, however, that a really fast tide is also a 'dead' period.

Many locals use light paternoster tackle with a long hook link, but a driftline fished deep often provides better sport. Baits as suggested for Mark 8. Pollack are also found in this area.

10 Evans Rock This is a mark for the more experienced boat angler. The rock lies at a depth of 5 fathoms about a mile out from the boat landing beach, with Durlston Head open of Peveril Point. It is sometimes marked in summer by lobster pot corks.

Legering with large cuttings of mackerel or herring on the outer fringes of the rock will often yield conger and dogfish. Deep driftlining is also rewarding, and a variety of species are taken on ragworm, mackerel strip and live prawn baits.

11 Peveril Ledge Pollack, wrasse, mackerel and occasional bass are taken near this submerged rocky ledge, which runs out to sea for ¼ mile from Peveril Point. A useful trolling route for the pollack is along the N side of the Point, starting near Swanage Pier and heading out to the can buoy marking the end of the ledge. Then put about and troll along the S side of the Point. Watch out for drying rocks, and do not attempt to hug the rocky ledge too close.

In addition to the species mentioned above, some good tope are taken off the end of the ledge, just beyond the buoy.

WARNING: At times a dangerous tide race appears off Peveril Point, particularly when the stream is flowing down-Channel. This is no place for novice boat anglers to visit without a local boatman. Experienced boat anglers should consult the tide table, and fish this mark when the stream is flowing up-Channel.

12 Anvil Point An excellent rock and wreck mark for pollack, black bream, conger, huss and pouting lies about 1 ¼ miles SE of Anvil Point Lighthouse. Fairly heavy leads are needed here, as the tide flows fast at times. Local knowledge is required to pin-point this mark, and holiday anglers should, in any case, only visit this area with an experienced boatman.

Boat Hire

Anglers wishing to fish in Swanage Bay can hire a suitable dinghy on the beach. These small craft are not allowed on the Peveril Point side of the pier because of the strong tides. Deep-sea trips can be arranged with local boatmen.

Local Baits

(Chart symbols are shown in brackets)

Prawns (PR) can be caught at low tide by working a hand-net among seaweed-covered rocks. However, owing to the very small tidal range the shore prawning at Swanage is not good, and local experience is needed to make a useful catch.

Better results can sometimes be obtained by working baited drop-nets from a dinghy over rough ground E of the pier. The best time for this is during the evening or when the water is cloudy.

Razorfish can be dug for limited periods during low spring tides.

Mackerel can be caught by trolling or feathering from a dinghy in the bay.

Tackle Dealers
Swanage Angling and Chandlery Centre,
6 High Street, Swanage.
Tel: 424989 (Tackle, chandlery, baits, etc.)

Swanage and District Angling Club
H.Q. next to the lifeboat station.

Chapman's Pool (See also Chart 5)

TIDES High water similar to Lulworth Cove. Tidal Streams: These become fairly strong soon after leaving the sheltering influence of Chapman's Pool, and the rate of flow increases very rapidly as St. Alban's Head is approached. Directly off the Head, about 1½ miles offshore, the tides attain a maximum rate at Springs of approximately 4¾ knots in both directions. A considerable tide race, with dangerous overfalls, may be encountered off the Head, and conditions are particularly bad when the tide is flowing hard against wind or swells. For small craft there is a narrow channel of comparatively quiet water close in to the rocks. Without local knowledge, however, persons in small undecked boats should only use this channel around slack water. (See Chart 5.)

TOPOGRAPHY A quiet, rock-flanked little bay, surrounded by imposing cliff scenery. A picturesque undercliff footpath leads S to several rocky float fishing spots under Emmetts Hill, and then climbs steeply to the summit of St. Alban's Head. A footpath also leads W over Hounstout Cliff, and along the coast to Kimmeridge.

Although launching a dinghy is quite easy at Chapman's Pool in normal weather conditions, this place cannot be recommended to the motorist-angler trailing his own boat. This is because the ground is very steep and slippery between the car park and the beach. When approaching by boat from the sea, a dinghy can be landed either at the gap where the stream runs out, or at the fisherman's hard on the SE side. The pool is encumbered with rocks, however, and very difficult to negotiate when a swell is running.

SHORE FISHING

1 Chapman's Pool Towards evening and after dark this can be a really 'bassy' spot, but beach casting is restricted owing to the snaggy bottom. The cleanest ground is found close to the gap where the stream runs out, but a survey during low spring tide, or from a dinghy when the water is clear, will reveal one or two other places where ground tackle can be used with accurate casting. In places it is possible to retrieve over the water-smoothed ledges of indurated clay, as described under **Kimmeridge,** Mark 7. The use of a spoon-shaped lead and fast-retrieve reel helps to prevent snagged tackle. Bass, conger and thornback rays are taken by this method. Recommended baits: large cuttings of fresh mackerel, frozen herring or squid.

From suitable rocky points it is possible to use sliding float tackle when weather conditions and tides permit. Pollack and wrasse are taken on prawn and ragworm baits. Evening is the best time for the pollack, and the bait should be kept on the move.

2 Freshwater Bay Considered by some local experts to be one of the best shore fishing spots along this stretch of coast, but it can only be reached by boat, or after nearly an hour's walk from Chapman's Pool. There is a small strip of beach here, mainly of coarse sand and shingle, backed by wave-washed cliffs of black clay which discolour the water. Some very good bass are taken on ground tackle, as well as large conger, rays, wrasse, etc. Fairly strong tackle is required, as fishing conditions are usually rough, the biggest curse being bottom weed.

Some float fishing is possible from nearby rocks when weather and tides permit, and this yields mainly pollack and wrasse. Baits as for Mark 1, Grey mullet are also very numerous here on occasions, especially when there is a lot of rotting seaweed lying on the beach. (See also remarks under **Kimmeridge,** Mark 7.)

BOAT FISHING

3 Emmetts Hill From just outside the S side of Chapman's

Pool entrance, there is useful inshore dinghy fishing as far as the gap where the undercliff path begins to climb towards St. Alban's Head. Slow drift-trolling (see under **Lulworth Cove Area,** Mark 9) takes mostly pollack, with the chance of an occasional bass. Also mackerel in season when using mackerel strip bait. Normal trolling takes all three species, according to the type of bait, lure, fishing depth and method of presentation.

It should be noted that on this side of St. Alban's Head the tide sets almost continuously towards the race, and boat anglers without local knowledge are advised not to fish S of Emmetts Hill. A reliable anchor or killick should always be carried, even when trolling.

Fishing at anchor produces good results from a number of points about 200 yards or so offshore. Driftlining yields pollack (sink and draw), bass and wrasse. Leger tackle takes conger, dogfish and – in some places – rays. Tight-lining with a monofil paternoster yields pouting and wrasse. Also conger and dogfish when the lower hook is fished close to the bottom on a flowing trace. Recommended baits: cuttings of mackerel or herring (conger, dogfish, rays, pouting); large squid cutting or head (conger); squid strip or tentacle (bass – drift-trolling); live prawn (bass, pollack, wrasse, pouting); ragworm (pollack, pouting, wrasse and – when driftlined, or trolled slowly with oars behind a suitable spoon – bass).

4 Ropehole Lake This mark lies close inshore, just off Ropehole Head – this being the first headland W of the flight of wooden steps leading down to the beach from the wooded Encombe Farm valley. It is an excellent spot for bass, which can be taken with a driftline baited with king ragworm, live prawn or herring strip. Slow drift-trolling takes pollack as well as bass. Conger, rays and wrasse are also found in the vicinity, and may be caught with the methods and baits described under Mark 3.

5 St. Alban's Ledge A rocky ledge, very steep-to in places, extends 2½ miles out to sea SW of St. Alban's Head, and there are numerous isolated rocky marks beyond this. The ledge is seldom fished by anglers owing to the strength of the tides, and the violent race, but it is the haunt of some very large pollack and conger; while a cod weighing 22lb was boated near here by a member of the Wareham and Purbeck Sea Angling Club.

This is definitely no place to fish in a dinghy or small motor launch, but during neap tides and settled weather it is well worth visiting this area with a fair-sized craft and a knowledgeable boatman.

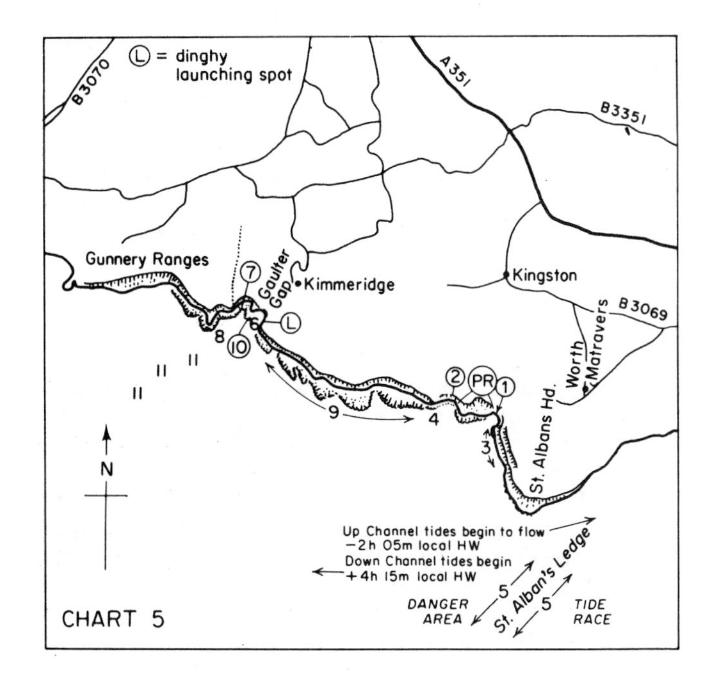

Local Baits

(Chart symbols are shown in brackets)

Prawns (P) of good size can be obtained sometimes by working baited drop-nets from a dinghy around rocky corners of the cove. The best catches are made in late summer and early autumn, when the water has been clouded by the sea washing against the local cliffs of black clay. Dusk, or a moonlit night, are also rewarding times, especially when the tide is falling.

Mackerel by trolling or feathering from a dinghy. Sometimes they can also be bought from the local professional fishermen.

Kimmeridge Bay (See also Chart 5)

TIDES Similar to Lulworth Cove, but see also cautionary remarks under Chapman's Pool.

TOPOGRAPHY Kimmeridge Bay is a quiet, uncommercialised cove about 1 mile from the village of Kimmeridge. It is reached by a private toll road (cars 15p), but there is free parking behind the beach. In reasonably good weather conditions the motorist-angler trailing his own boat will experience no difficulty in getting afloat on the E side of the bay. Shore anglers should note that the coast immediately W of Kimmeridge, as far as Lulworth Cove, forms part of a W.D. gunnery range, and is closed to the public for most of the year.

SHORE FISHING

6 East Side Some rock fishing can be carried on from suitable vantage points when weather and tides permit. Pollack are likely to be encountered towards evening, using float-spinning tactics and ragworm bait. Wrasse, bass and grey mullet are also present, and big tope have been caught from the boat slipway.

7 Sharnel This beach can be reached by walking W from Gaulter Gap along the top of a low cliff for nearly a mile. The upper half of the beach consists of shingle, but below half-tide level the pebbles give way to shallow ledges of smooth and *very slippery* black rock.

Below low water level, these gently sloping ledges in turn dip beneath sandy patches of sea-bed. Thus, by careful positioning and accurate casting, it is possible to send out a monofil paternoster on to patches of clean ground; afterwards retrieving the tackle over the smooth ledge of rock. Drifting bottom weed can be a curse here at times, but it is worth persevering because this spot is capable of yielding some very good bass. A spoon-shaped lead helps to reduce the risk of snagged tackle. Some conger are also taken. Evening fishing is recommended, beginning during the early flood. A reasonably stiff rod is essential here. Recommended baits: large cuttings of mackerel, herring and squid, ragworm.

Mr. W. H. Hilton, a Wareham angler who often fishes this spot, declares that at times this stretch of shore is visited by really large grey mullet – some of them potential record-breakers. On rising tides, particularly at Springs, huge shoals sometimes come within inches of the shore, feeding on the maggots and other forms of life in the rotting banks of weed. 'Occasionally,' Mr. Hilton told me, 'I have seen this decaying weed piled nearly 4ft high, with the tide lapping it, and the mullet grovelling in it like pigs, with their tail-fins right out of the water!'

8 Broad Bench A little W of Mark 7 the shoreline becomes strewn with boulders, and curves S towards a low promontory called Broad Bench Point. Here, for several hours either side of low water, a platform-shaped ledge provides useful fishing spots. The deepest water will be found on the E side, near the seaward end. Weed is the main problem, but guidance from a local angler, or careful prospecting at low water (preferably Springs), will enable float tackle to be fished fairly deep. (See also under **Weymouth,** Mark 15). Wrasse are taken here by day; pollack mainly from early evening until dusk. There is also a chance of encountering the occasional bass. In a few *comparatively* clear spots it is also possible to use bottom tackle for conger, but the gear must be sturdy enough to get the conger off the bottom immediately after striking.

Broad Bench has almost vertical quay-like sides, and the top is flat, with shallow rock pools here and there. The footing is safe – not slippery like most rock stances in this area.

Baits: prawns, ragworm, sea-slaters (wrasse, pollack, bass); mackerel or herring strips (pollack, bass). Note: Prawns can sometimes be found in the Broad Bench tide pools – provided one catches them before the gulls and sea anemones! These prawns are small, however, and should be bunched on the hook.

BOAT FISHING

9 Kimmeridge Ledges A series of rocky ledges jut out from the shore, commencing just outside the E entrance to Kimmeridge Bay and continuing almost as far as Chapman's Pool. About midway between these two points, the ledges and isolated rocks dry for up to ½ mile offshore at LW Springs, and the whole area must be fished with caution. On no account should it be approached during a period of heavy swells.

This stretch of coast yields good pollack, which can be taken by drifting or slow drift-trolling, as described under **Lulworth Cove Area,** Mark 9. Early morning and evening are the best times for this; while mackerel and occasional bass may also be taken. Wrasse, conger and dogfish are caught by the usual methods.

10 Kimmeridge Bay For a small rowing dinghy there is quite good fishing in Kimmeridge Bay itself, especially towards evening. Slow trolling yields pollack and occasional bass. It should be noted that there are a number of rocks in the bay, some of which dry at low water. Others can be seen when the water is clear, and fishing at anchor near these rocks may produce conger, dogfish, wrasse, pollack, bass etc. Methods and baits as recommended under **Chapman's Pool,** Mark 3.

11 Broad Bench Point There are some good rock marks directly off this promontory, between one-third and ½ mile offshore. Driftlining with live prawns, king ragworm or fish strips (worked sink and draw) produces some good pollack. Bottom fishing with fish baits takes conger and huss. Also wrasse on worm or shellfish baits.

There are several other good rocky marks in the area, and these may often be located by lobster pot corks.

Local Baits

Prawns can sometimes be caught in baited drop-nets worked from Broad Bench or a dinghy. This is only worthwhile when the water is dirty after a 'blow', or after dusk has fallen.

Sea Slaters are plentiful on the E side of Broad Bench Point. They are found near the high tide mark, and seem to favour boulders resting on patches of the local oil-bearing shale. Turn over a small, flat-shaped boulder and dozens scamper out, but you'll be lucky to pick up two before they all disappear under the next stone. However, on turning over this stone many will return with equal alacrity to the stone previously overturned, and so it goes on. Indeed, if you place your hand flat on the beach, leaving a slight space, the chances are that half a dozen will run under it!.

These slaty-black, woodlice-like creatures are a reasonably good float fishing bait for wrasse, school bass and inshore pollack. I have also used the smaller ones for mullet with some success.

Lulworth Cove Area (See also Chart 6)

TIDES HW: + 5h 07m London Bridge. Rise: 7ft at Springs; 4½ ft at Neaps. There are no currents of any consequence within the cove, but outside the tidal streams run fairly strongly, and at times a rowing boat would be unable to make any headway against them. Maximum rate at Springs off Lulworth Cove approaches 2 knots during both ebb and flood.

TOPOGRAPHY Lulworth Cove is a remarkable bowl-shaped inlet, about a mile in circumference, and surrounded by tall, greyish-white cliffs. With its strangely contorted rock strata, and its fossil forest of long-extinct trees, it is possibly the most picturesque and interesting spot on the Dorset coast.

Downland and cliff tracks lead W from the cove to Durdle Door and White Nothe, and the scenery in this direction is superb. To the E of Lulworth, unfortunately, a long stretch of coast, downland and heath has been taken over by the War Department for use as a gunnery range, and access is prohibited for most of the year, with the exception of August and public holiday periods. However, we have included details of the fishing along this 'forbidden' coastline in the hope that some day it will once again become available to the public.

SHORE FISHING

1 Lulworth Beach The beach inside Lulworth Cove is mainly of steeply shelving pebbles. During the summer months the water on the W side of the cove is much disturbed by swimmers and boats, and even after dark there is a risk of distance casters fouling the boat moorings.

The E side of the cove is usually quieter, but here the sea-bed becomes progressively more snaggy with rocks and weed. The best plan, therefore, is to fish at night at selected points on the N or NE shore, using a monofil paternoster. If this is weighted with a spoon-shaped lead the risk of snagging will be considerably reduced. Catches consist mainly of pouting and conger, but some good bass of 9-11lb have also been taken in the late evening and after dark.

Recommended baits: large cuttings of mackerel, frozen herring and squid.

2 Lulworth Rocks Sliding float tackle, adjusted to suit the state of tide, can be used from the rocky ledge at the E side of the cove entrance. This is only possible in reasonably calm conditions, and preferably when the tide is flowing down-Channel. (See tidal data on Chart 6). The species taken by this method include wrasse, pollack, and occasionally bass and mackerel. Recommended baits: ragworm and live prawns (wrasse, pollack, bass); mackerel slip (bass, mackerel and – sometimes – pollack). One successful bass angler who fishes these rocks makes a point of groundbaiting with pieces of chopped-up herring before commencing to fish.

Grey mullet are also found here quite often, and can be taken with quill float tackle.

The rocky ledge on the W side of the cove can be fished by the same methods, and is a rewarding spot – especially when the tide is flowing up-Channel. However, access is by a steep and difficult path down the 'backbone' of the cliff, and holiday anglers would be unwise to attempt to fish here unless accompanied by a local.

3 Mupes Bay Being well sheltered from the W this bay makes an ideal fishing spot when a SW gale is blowing. Unfortunately, it lies within the limits of the War Department ranges. Bass are taken here, and while this book was being written a magnificent specimen of 13lb 2oz was caught on squid bait by a holiday angler. Leger tackle is recommended, and this also stands a good chance of taking pouting, conger, huss and rays. Baits as for Mark 1.

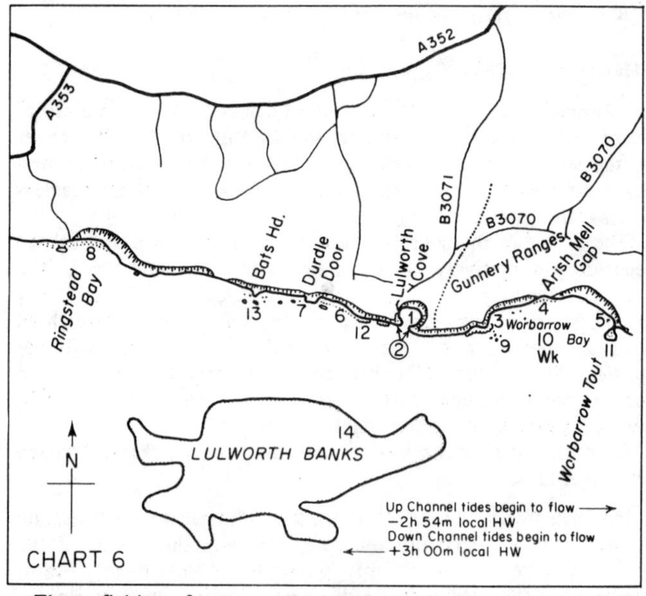

CHART 6

Float fishing from nearby rocks has also accounted for pollack, wrasse and occasional bass. Baits as for Mark 2. Grey mullet have been taken on light quill float tackle.

4 Arish Mell Gap This used to be a good shore fishing spot for rays, huss and pouting, but there is little hope of it ever becoming available again to holiday anglers. It lies within the limits of the gunnery ranges, and is also the site of an outfall for radioactive effluent from the Winfrith Atomic Research Establishment.

5 Worbarrow Bay The E end of Worbarrow Bay is a very good fishing spot – particularly in late summer and autumn. Bass, conger, rays, huss, pouting and tope have all been caught in the cove, but as it lies inside the gunnery ranges most visiting anglers will only be able to fish here during the periods around

Easter, Whitsun and in August when this coast is opened to the public.

When weather conditions are suitable there is excellent rock fishing from the nearby promontory known as Worbarrow Tout – but one has to get well out on to the point. Bass and pollack are plentiful, and are taken on sliding float or spinner. The locals favour a *large* and lively ragworm when using float, and a plastic sandeel for spinning. Wrasse and grey mullet are also taken by the usual methods, and some nice bream are found here at times.

6 St. Oswald's Bay This fine stretch of sandy beach usually has a moderate run of surf, and offers plenty of scope for the shore caster. It is not nearly so crowded as Lulworth Cove in summer, and daytime fishing presents no difficulties. However, a late evening visit is usually much more rewarding. The bay is most conveniently approached from Lulworth Cove, taking the tarred lane which leads W uphill out of the cove. This soon degenerates into a footpath which wanders down to St. Oswald's Beach.

The sands are flanked at either end by outcrops of rock, and bass are taken by casting out leger or monofil paternoster tackle on to clean ground about midway along the beach. In addition, dogfish are taken here, as well as conger when fishing close to the rocks. Baits as for Mark 1.

The rocks at the extreme end of the bay yield bass by spinning, but care must be taken not to get cut off by rising tides.

7 Durdle Door This is a fairly deep bay of fine shingle. It is a good spot for bass, conger, pouting, dogfish and occasional ray, which are taken mainly on leger tackle and fish baits. In addition, quite a few specialist anglers have caught decent-sized tope here. Tackle varies for this type of fishing, but one useful set-up consists of a 4ft trace of flexible plastic-covered wire carrying a 5/0 hook. The trace is attached by a strong swivel clip to the reel line, on which slides a free-running leger lead. Fish baits are used, and many tope anglers fishing from the shore favour a large piece of frozen herring. This, on the 5/0 hook, is also well within the capabilities of any large bass, conger or huss which may be around. Mackerel (especially the small 'harvest' mackerel) are also good; while freshly-caught pouting or poor cod, though perhaps not quite so good, are worth using.

It should be mentioned that most tope insist on a tidy-looking bait, and that as little as possible of the hook should be visible. Whether or not the barb should be left exposed is a controversial point, but it if *is* hidden it should be buried only very lightly, and slanted so that it pulls clear of the bait as soon as the strike is made.

The bite of a tope is very light, and the fish will quickly drop the bait if it feels any suspicious resistance or movement of the line. If your reel has a powerful check, it is best to leave this off, using instead a very slight pressure from the drag. Whatever the type of reel, it must carry plenty of line – although this need not be very heavy. When using a reasonably lively rod, it should be possible to beat even the largest tope with about 300 yards of 25lb b.s. line. Tope often run far and fast when they feel the hook, and if pressure is applied too soon the fish will almost certainly be lost.

8 Ringstead Bay This is a good shore fishing beach beneath the lofty chalk headland of White Nothe, but as the sea-bed is snaggy in many places it is advisable to use a spoon-shaped lead and fast-retrieve reel. The fish caught here include large conger, bass, bream, pouting, cod and whiting, according to season. One favourite fishing area lies about three-quarters of the way along the E beach. Recommended baits include ragworm, lug, and cuttings of mackerel and squid. For large conger (they have been taken here up to 40lb) try a squid head on a 5/0 hook, fished after dark.

Fishing from local rocks with fine tackle has also yielded some good grey mullet. One visiting angler took three weighing 6lb, 5lb, and 3½lb from here, baiting with bread paste.

BOAT FISHING

WARNING: Due to navigational restrictions, Marks 9, 10 and 11 should not be fished when firing is in progress on the Lulworth Firing Ranges. Up-to-date information on these restrictions is obtainable from local Coastguards. Normally the ranges are not in use for six days at Easter, five days at Whitsun, all of August, and 14 days at Christmas.

9 Mupe Rocks These wave-washed rocks are situated a short distance offshore at the W end of Worbarrow Bay. Pollack and bass are to be caught here, and a useful method is to bait up a lightly leaded flowing trace with a live prawn, ragworm or frozen sandeel, and then alternately drift and row just outside the rocks with the tide. Bass and pollack are also taken by trolling *quietly* with a 'Red Gill' sandeel.

Besides trolling around the rocky headland, good results are also obtained sometimes by trolling slowly and fairly deep *across* the tide, working outwards from Mupe Rocks for about

½ mile, keeping the centre of the rocks in line with the centre of the headland behind. Increase the trolling depth gradually on the outward journey, and reduce it when returning inshore.

Legering at anchor with fish baits near Mupe Rocks will take conger and huss. Driftlining with ragworm, prawns and mackerel strips yields pouting and pollack; also wrasse when using prawns and ragworm. Sink and draw tactics will often stimulate bites.

10 Worbarrow Bay Several marks in this bay, including a wreck, at one time provided good fishing for pollack, conger, huss, skate, pouting and wrasse. An outfall for radioactive effluent discharges into the sea near here, but so far the fish do not seem to have been contaminated.

11 Worbarrow Tout Another excellent area for pollack and bass, which can be caught by the methods described under Mark 9. A useful trolling or drifting route extends from a point about ¼ mile W of the Tout, and this can be followed close in past the Tout, and *fairly* close in under Gad Cliff to a point about halfway to Brandy Bay. Watch out for two drying rocks under the cliff, though.

12 Dungy Head This mark is mentioned here mainly because it is easily reached from Lulworth Cove. A useful trolling area for pollack, particularly on a quiet summer or autumn evening. Mackerel may also be taken on a spinner in late summer, and drifting or slow trolling (see Mark 9) with sandeel or a suitable ragworm-baited spoon has also been known to take the occasional bass. Legering yields conger and dogfish; driftlining yields wrasse, pouting and pollack.

13 Bats Head This mark derives its name from a distinctive chalk cliff on the nearby coast. Two wave-washed rocks a little way offshore are known as the Cow and Calf, and this area produces bass, mackerel, huss, wrasse and pouting by the methods described under Mark 12. Also some pollack, but these are mostly small.

14 Lulworth Banks This fairly extensive bank lies from 2-4 miles SW of Lulworth Cove, and small outboard-powered craft would be well advised to limit their fishing here to neap tide periods, during settled weather. The nature of the sea-bed varies considerably over the banks, but the part nearest the cove possesses several patches of rock and broken ground, which are often marked with lobster pot corks in summer. Black bream, thornback rays, conger, pollack, pouting, wrasse, cod, whiting and many other species are found here, depending on the season.

To reach this area, head out of Lulworth Cove, and then keep the flagstaff on Bindon Hill in line with the end of the rocky spur jutting out at the W side of the cove entrance. One is getting near the fishing ground when Arish Mell Gap begins to appear beyond the headland *inside* Mupe Rocks. (Note: Arish Mell Gap more or less divides the cliffy shores of Worbarrow Bay in the centre.)

There are some good thornback ray marks over the banks – one rewarding area being about 2½ miles offshore, due S of Hembury Tout. Tope also roam the banks, and the S side is visited by flatfish, including some good turbot at certain seasons.

BOAT HIRE

Deep-sea fishing trips are best arranged at Weymouth.

Local Baits

Prawns can sometimes be obtained by working baited drop-nets from a dinghy close in to the Dungy Head rocks. Catches are best around dusk in late summer and early autumn when the tide is falling. It is useless to try when the sun is shining and the water is clear.

Mackerel can often be caught in summer by trolling, or by feathering from a drifting dinghy. They can also be bought at times from the local professional fishermen.

Ragworm are present in areas of mixed stones and mud inside Lulworth Cove, but they are very localized and can only be dug for a brief period during low tides.

Weymouth and Portland (See also Chart 7)

TIDES HW: + 5h 05m London Bridge. Rise: 6¾ ft at Springs; 4¼ ft at Neaps. Tidal Streams: There are no dangerous currents in the bay within 2-3 miles of the harbour, but farther out the tide sets with increasing strength towards the notorious Portland Race. This area of roaring overfalls is the most dangerous tide race on the south coast, and it is caused by the fierce south-going streams on both sides of Portland Bill meeting the up-Channel and down-Channel streams. Rocky ledges rising abruptly from the sea-bed off the Bill add to the violence and confusion of the race. Considerable respect must therefore be paid to strong offshore winds blowing in the direction of the race, and a reliable anchor should always be carried as a safeguard against drifting in that direction in the event of engine failure, etc.

TOPOGRAPHY Weymouth is a sizeable holiday resort, with a sandy beach that provides safe swimming. A good deep-water harbour is situated in the river, the mouth of which is sheltered by two long piers. Unfortunately this harbour becomes very crowded with cruising craft during the summer months, and at times below the Town Bridge it is difficult to find a place to land and tie up. In this event small craft without masts are advised to head further up-river into the Backwater.

A very beautiful stretch of coast lies to the E of Weymouth, with downland cliff walks from Osmington Mills to Lulworth Cove. Immediately to the W is Portland Naval Harbour and the rugged Portland Peninsula.

SHORE FISHING

As a rule shore fishing is best during the flood tide, or round about slack high water, Also, at bass or conger marks, night fishing is usually much more rewarding than daytime fishing.

The so-called Pleasure Pier, beyond the British Railways Steamer Berth, is NOT recommended for fishing – despite the fact that it is much frequented by visiting anglers.

1 Stone Pier This is the breakwater which guards the entrance to Weymouth Harbour on its S (Portland) side. From Weymouth sea-front it can be reached by crossing the river by the Town Bridge, and then turning down the waterfront past the Lifeboat Station, and along the Nothe Walk. Sliding float tackle, adjusted to suit the species and state of tide, will take mackerel and pollack. The best time for pollack is when high water arrives towards evening; the best bait is ragworm, which for preference should be kept on the move by repeatedly casting and retrieving. For mackerel the best bait is mackerel slip. Bass may also be encountered here on occasions.

Flatfish are sometimes taken by casting a ragworm-baited leger or monofil paternoster on to sandy ground on the inside of the pier, and whiting are liable to put in an appearance towards evening during late autumn and winter.

At night, strong ground tackle baited with large cuttings of squid, mackerel or herring may yield conger from the outer (Portland) side of the pier.

Mullet are also caught, usually very early in the morning, from the two small jetties which jut out into the harbour near the beginning of the Stone Pier.

2 Weymouth Harbour and Backwater Although ignored by

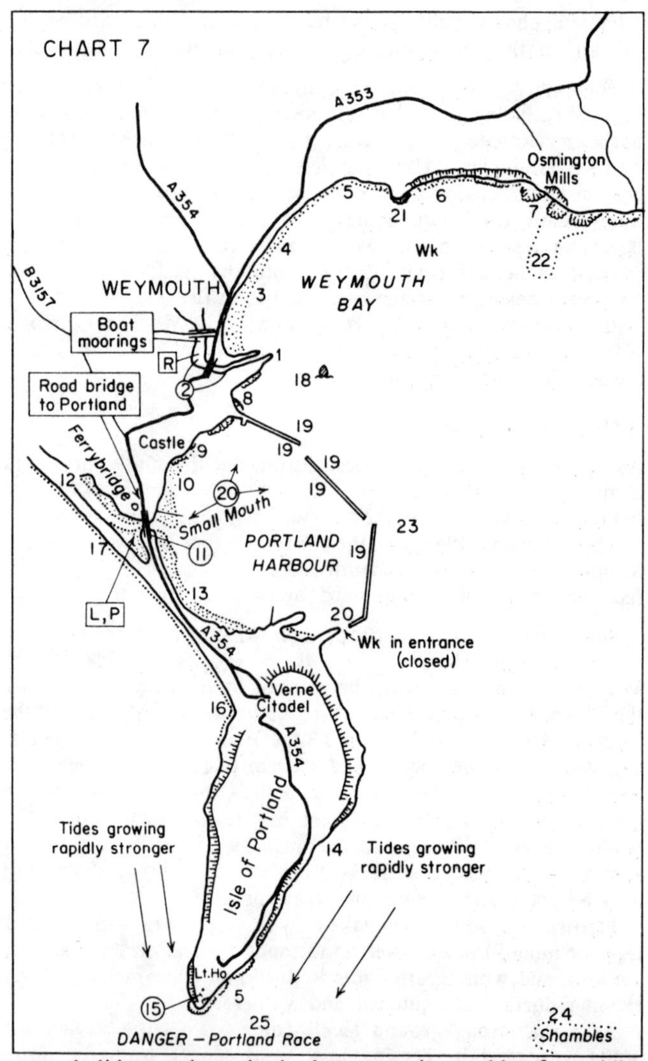

many holiday anglers, the harbour area is capable of providing fair sport. It is, however, best fished in the early morning, or towards evening, when boat traffic is not so active. Conger of quite good size are present at several places, and can be taken on strong leger tackle baited with herring, mackerel, squid, etc. The S side, in the Nothe area, is well worth prospecting.

Grey mullet are also present, both in the harbour and the pool above the bridge known as the Backwater. One young holiday angler caught over two dozen on light river tackle, the heaviest fish weighing 4lb 13oz. Indeed, mulleting is the ideal sport for the inland angler holidaying by the sea, if he has only light freshwater tackle.

WARNING: Leger tackle should only be lobbed out a yard or two from the quays. If cast out any distance it is likely to get snagged on the numerous boat moorings. For this reason float tackle is widely used in the harbour area.

3 Weymouth Beach Although crowded with bathers by day during the holiday season, this can be a useful night fishing area for bass – especially when a SE wind is bringing in a run of surf. Use leger tackle or a monofil paternoster baited with large cuttings of fresh-caught mackerel, frozen herring or squid. The stretch of shore N of the Pier Bandstand is most likely to produce results. Flounders are also found here, and when daytime fishing, some anglers prefer to use two-hook tackle, baiting one smaller hook with ragworm or lugworm.

4 Overcombe Beach This is a quieter stretch of beach on the NE outskirts of Weymouth. Bass are taken by methods described under Mark 3.

5 Bowleze Cove Another useful shore fishing area, much frequented in summer by anglers holidaying at nearby caravan camps. Rocks, mostly submerged, encumber the sea-bed close inshore on either side of the mouth of the stream, and this necessitates care in casting. However, the prawns and other small marine creatures inhabiting this reef attract bass to the area, and despite the risk of losing some tackle it is worth fishing as close to the rocks as possible. A spoon-shaped lead and fast-retrieve reel helps to prevent snags. Conger, too, are found here.

Fishing is best at night, and the use of fairly large hooks is recommended, baited with generous cuttings of squid, fresh-caught mackerel or frozen herring. By day in summer the beach gets very crowded. In sandy areas one can also expect dabs, flounders and soles on the usual baits.

6 Redcliff Beach Various species of fish are taken from this shingly beach, which has rocky areas at either end. The E end is considered best by many local anglers, and catches include pollack, mackerel, pouting, bass, rays and wrasse. Night fishing gives the best results, with mackerel and herring baits taking the bass, conger, huss and rays, as well as the larger pouting.

Single-hook leger tackle is recommended for most of these species. A small whole pouting also makes a good conger bait. Ragworm baits take wrasse (mostly by day) and pouting. King ragworm are quite good for bass, and squid excellent. Spinning for bass, mackerel and pollack is also productive, and in calm weather there is scope for light float fishing for mullet near the E end of the beach.

7 Osmington Mills This picturesque longshore hamlet is a pleasant and rewarding fishing spot for bass, conger, huss and pouting, but the shore is very snaggy with ledges and boulders. When ground fishing it is best to use a spoon-shaped lead (see Mark 5 above), and a suitable place for this lies a few yards E of the waterfall, Accurate casting is essential, and it helps considerably to make a low-tide inspection.

8 Newtons Cove A useful shore fishing spot between the Stone Pier (Mark 1) and the N breakwater of Portland Harbour. Catches include conger, bass, pollack and mullet near the rocky areas (including the old Nothe Fort); whilst flatfish are an added bonus on sandy ground. The N side of the cove is rocky and bottom tackle will be lost here. Float fishing and spinning are a much better proposition. There are also some rocks elsewhere, and a preliminary low-tide survey is recommended. Once the angler has got his bearings, however, this can be a good night fishing spot. Baits as recommended under Mark 6.

The SW side of the cove is formed by the approach to the N Breakwater of Portland Harbour. The shoreline here is fringed with tumbled blocks of Portland stone. The breakwater itself is out of bounds to civilians, but about 100 yards outside the boundary of the Admiralty property there are one or two places where it is possible to cast out ground tackle. One useful spot is just opposite a square manhole cover in the road. Cast straight out on to clear ground, and when retrieving reel in briskly so that the sinker swims over obstructions close inshore.

9 Bincleaves and Sandsfoot Odd though it may seem, this popular fishing and yachting area lies inside Portland Naval Harbour. Bass, conger and flounders are taken here, depending on the nature of the bottom, which is very variable. Bincleaves beach (shingly sand) fishes best during onshore winds, with bass and conger the main species.

Bass also feed fairly close inshore at Castle Cove, between the jetty and Sandsfoot Castle, but during the summer months there is a good deal of yachting activity here, so this area is best fished after dark. From autumn to about mid-winter is often the most

Shorecasting sport reaches its peak after dark along the majority of Dorset beaches. However, to obtain consistent results it is essential to pinpoint the most likely feeding areas, and to fish them at the right stages of the tide.

A "gull's-eye" view of the Chesil Beach from Portland's West Weare cliffs. This remarkable bank of wave-rounded shingle is noted for its shore fishing potential. It stretches unbroken to Bridport Harbour, some 17 miles distant.

Black bream are encountered at several localised boat marks along the Dorset coast, from Swanage to Lyme Bay. In some seasons they run to a very good average size. This specimen was taken while dinghy fishing about 2½ miles out in Lyme Bay.

Winter shore fishing near the lighthouse at Portland Bill. Just around the corner beyond the lighthouse is Pulpit rock and some adjoining platform-shaped fishing positions which often produce good results.

productive period. Baits include lugworm (they can be dug locally), king ragworm, mackerel strip and squid.

10 Rylands Lane-End At the end of this road an archway under the railway track gives access to a sandy patch of shore bounded by rocks. It is a good spot for bass – particularly in the autumn.

11 Ferrybridge This is the name given to the area where the road bridge to Portland spans the narrow channel of tidal water linking Portland Harbour with the Fleet backwater. Ground tackle cast out at various points will take bass, conger and flounders. Baits as for Mark 9. At the site of the demolished railway bridge, there are some rocks which provide a stance for float fishing for bass; also ground fishing for conger. Fishing from the road bridge is neither convenient nor safe.

12 Littlesea There are several places in the Littlesea area where shore fishing is possible. Bass and flatfish can be taken by casting out a leger or monofil paternoster from the lugworm grounds on the W side of the road bridge. Early flood, around evening, is a good time for this.

The writer has also taken bass on float tackle from the Littlesea tide-run during the flood and early ebb. This was on the Chesil Beach side, near the W end of the tide-run just before it widens out to form the E Fleet. The bait in this instance was bunched ragworms, and it was cast straight out and allowed to drift away on the tide. Finally a slow retrieve was made, and the cast repeated.

13 Harbour – West Side The road and abandoned railway track enter the Isle of Portland side by side. On the Portland Harbour side of the old railway track there is a beach, and light bottom fishing here takes bass, flounders and the occasional plaice. Baits as for Mark 9. Cars can be left in a nearby car park on the Littlesea side of the road. Fishing is best here during the last two hours of the flood tide.

14 Church Ope Cove This sandy cove, flanked by rocks. lies below ruined Rufus Castle. It offers good scope for the beach-caster, and night fishing with leger tackle often yields conger and bass. Some plaice and soles are also taken. Due to snaggy ground close in, it is advisable to use a spoon-shaped lead and a fast-retrieve reel. There are also float fishing possibilities in this area. Family anglers will find this a pleasant spot for a fishing picnic.

15 Portland Bill Area During reasonably calm conditions there is excellent rock fishing around the S extremity of the Portland Peninsula. Owing to the nature of the local rock strata, the sea has eroded many of these fishing rocks into natural platforms, and from these it is possible to catch bass, pollack, mackerel and garfish on sliding float tackle. Baits commonly used for this type of fishing include strips of fresh mackerel and frozen sandeels, but best of all are small live sand smelts and tiny wrasse, which can often be caught on the spot with light tackle. Some of the local bass specialists, when using these livebaits, keep them in a plastic bucket filled with sea water, with a small battery-operated aquarium air pump to keep the water aerated.

The tides run very strongly around Portland Bill, creating the notorious Portland Race only a short distance offshore. It is these powerful tidal currents which govern the feeding habits and routine of the local bass and other predators, and rock fishing results in this area are usually best during the last hour of the flood and the early stages of the ebb – particularly if this period also coincides with sunrise or dusk.

At selected vantage points near the Bill it is also possible, around the HW period, to use the set of the tidal streams to carry one's baited float tackle well offshore in the general direction of the Race. This is where the really big bass are often to be encountered.

Wrasse may also be taken on lug-baited float tackle set to fish deep near the kelp beds, but the largest specimens are generally taken on single-hook bottom tackle baited with hardbacked crab. However, the bottom is nearly always very snaggy, so one must be prepared to lose some tackle. It is essential to use a disposable sinker attached to the main trace by a short length of weaker line.

Both wrasse and pollack will try to seek refuge in weed or rocks as soon as they are hooked, and require firm handling from the very outset. The teeth of wrasse are sharp, so examine your trace for damage after landing a big one. Wrasse are taken fairly close in to the rocks, and fairly deep. The interest of pollack can often be stimulated by 'float-spinning' – casting the float well out, and then retrieving slowly.

Pollack, bass and mackerel can also be taken in this area by spinning. A favourite artificial lure for the bass and pollack is a 'Red Gill' plastic sandeel presented about 2 to 3ft behind a Wye lead. Mackerel, on the other hand, are more conveniently taken with a small silvery metal spoon or pirk with sufficient built-in weight to make the use of an up-trace lead unnecessary. Suitable lures in this category include the ABU 'Krill', small 'Koster' or Intrepid 'Flectolite'. All these have the added merit of possessing a well-proved appeal for bass and pollack.

Some very large conger lurk around Portland, particularly in those areas where quarry waste has been tipped into the sea, thereby providing these giant eels with a wonderful selection of rocky lairs. Such places are, of course, very snaggy, but there are certain spots known to local anglers where strong ground tackle can be risked with a reasonable chance of success. Even so, tackle losses are heavy, and as a rule old nuts and bolts are used as disposable sinkers. A strong gaff, a reliable companion, and a sack for the catch, are vital for this type of fishing. The best time to contact the big conger is after dark, but this requires caution and a powerful headband lamp which leaves both hands free for playing and landing a big conger.

16 Chesil Cove This shingly cove lies at the E extremity of the Chesil Beach, where it curves round to join the Isle of Portland. Bass, conger and pouting are the species most commonly taken; while cod and whiting are sometimes caught in late autumn and winter. A Wessex leger trace does well here when baited with large cuttings of squid, mackerel or frozen herring. Night fishing gives the best results.

17 Adelaide This very useful stretch of fishing beach is so called in memory of the East Indiaman, 'Royal Adelaide', which was wrecked here many years ago. It was, in fact, a double tragedy, because that same night the local fishermen got hold of some kegs of spirits from the wreck. There, on the beach, they proceeded to make merry; and there in the darkness, as they fell into a drunken stupor, several were swept away by the waves and drowned.

To reach this ill-fated but rewarding fishing spot, park the car in the public car park just S of the road bridge connecting Portland with the mainland. It is then only a few minutes walk on to the Chesil Beach.

The beach along this stretch is very steep-to, and even anglers who are not very proficient at distance casting will be able to get their tackle out into several fathoms of water. The species taken include bass, dogfish and flatfish; also mackerel by spinning, and some cod in autumn and winter. In addition, this area has on occasions yielded large tope, and quite a few night anglers have been broken by unidentified 'monsters'. It would seem that many fish, including deep-water species, are diverted close inshore by the out-jutting Portland Peninsula. This last remark applies also to Mark 16.

Useful Shore Fishing References

Spinning for mackerel. See under **Chesil Beach**, Mark 1.

BOAT FISHING

18 Sewer Buoy A sewer runs out from the SE side of the Nothe, mainly over a reef of seaweedy rocks. The outer end of the sewer is marked by a buoy, situated about ½ mile ESE of the Stone Pier.

Bass and pollack may be taken in this vicinity by drifting slowly in a dinghy, and giving a quiet pull on the oars every few seconds to keep the line streamed astern. Use a long, fine trace. Two baits which have proved successful here are live prawn and small live wrasse. Ragworm is also good, and this is sometimes more effective when presented behind a baby spinner. Big conger, too, are taken among the shallow reefs.

19 Portland Breakwaters The massive stone breakwaters forming Portland Harbour extend for approximately three miles, and below the waterline they are built of huge tumbled blocks of stone. This method of construction has produced a mini-labyrinth of kelp-fronded crevices, providing ideal cover for prawns, crabs, blennies, wrasse, tiny pouting and many other forms of small marine life. Needless to say, this all adds up to a wealth of food for large predatory fish, and many a big conger has its lair beneath these breakwaters. Best bait for these powerful sea eels is a large fillet of freshly caught mackerel, or a whole small squid, presented on a strong 7/0 hook to wire.

Bass, too, come nosing in around the stonework in search of prawns and small crabs. There are three entrances to Portland Harbour (one of them being partly blocked by a wreck) and obviously any bass entering or leaving the harbour must do so through one of these gaps in the breakwaters. Plenty of large bass are captured by dinghy anglers using the set of the tidal stream to driftline a live prawn towards the entrance. Care must be taken to avoid obstructing the NE and E entrances which are used by Naval vessels, but the blocked southern entrance is used only by small fishing craft. A supply of prawns for bait can be caught either in Portland Harbour itself, or in the adjoining Littlesea area.

Another popular method for these bass is slow trolling close alongside the breakwater with a plastic sandeel, or some other suitable lure. Trolling under sail can be particularly killing, due to the absence of engine disturbance, but it calls for extra care when the wind is flukey because any sudden loss of speed could lose you your lure on the very snaggy bottom.

A third method – and in many ways the most attractive one – is float fishing from an anchored boat. The bait is set about 8ft below the float, and then allowed to drift away with the tide until it reaches a bassy hotspot. Here again you can bait up with a live prawn or, alternatively, you can use a small live pouting or wrasse. These small fish can be caught close to the breakwater and are specially attractive to large bass. They can be presented by lightly passing one point of a medium-sized treble hook through the back, between the head and the leading edge of the dorsal fin.

WARNING: Besides taking care not to obstruct the harbour entrances used by Naval vessels, boat anglers should also note that anchoring is forbidden within 100ft of the N breakwater – i.e. the section between Bincleaves Beach and the N harbour entrance. Landing on the harbour breakwater is also forbidden by the Admiralty.

20 Portland Harbour Bass, pollack, mullet, conger, wrasse, flounders and plaice are caught inside Portland Harbour. Driftlining from an anchored boat, using a live prawn as bait, yields bass in the tideflow near Ferrybridge.

NOTE: **Bass Nursery Area.** Boat fishing for bass is prohibited in the Fleet (west of Ferrybridge) throughout the year.

Conger are found near the breakwaters and certain submerged obstructions. Some larger conger also inhabit the wreck which blocks the S entrance to the harbour.

Large mullet are plentiful in the harbour, and they can be taken on light float tackle and size 10 – 12 hooks. Bread for groundbait and hook baits usually gives best results.

Flatfish can be taken on light leger tackle, with a small cigar-shaped "crab-beater" float positioned about 8 inches above the hook to lift the bait off the bottom. Baits: ragworm and lugworm. The baited-spoon method also produces results. The W side of the harbour, to the N and S of Small Mouth, is a rewarding area, and reasonably clear of moorings and other obstructions.

WARNING: Boat anglers fishing the Small Mouth area should note that at times the tide runs swiftly under the bridge at Ferrybridge. As there is very little headroom, a masted craft can easily be capsized if carried there by the current.

21 Redcliff Point This mark lies about 2 miles from Weymouth Harbour, and in normal weather conditions is within easy range of an outboard dinghy. The best catches are made on rocky or 'ledgy' ground about 400 – 600 yards offshore from the headland. The methods most commonly employed are legering (conger, huss and rays), driftline (pouting, wrasse, and occasional bass and small pollack); drifting (pouting, small pollack and bass); slow trolling (bass, small pollack and mackerel). Baits: cuttings of mackerel and herring (conger, huss, skate, pouting); live prawns (bass, pollack, pouting, wrasse, thornback skate); ragworm (pollack, pouting, wrasse, bass).

22 Ringstead Ledge Species, methods and baits similar to Mark 21, but the fish often run to a better size. This mark is about 3 miles from Weymouth Harbour, and should not be attempted by small craft when fresh or strong winds are likely from the SW, as the return journey may prove difficult.

23 Skate Grounds Some excellent skate and rays are caught quite close inshore in the bay. One good area lies just beyond the 'Chequer' Fort on Portland Breakwater, about ¼ mile out, where the tide sweeps round the corner. The current is very strong here at times. Dogfish are also taken in this area.

24 The Shambles Bank This steep-to bank of sand and broken shells yields some fine turbot on occasions, although it is only fair to add that catches have dwindled in recent years – probably due to over-fishing by trawlers. The mark lies dangerously close to the Portland Race, and for visiting anglers the guidance of a competent local boatman is absolutely essential. Other species taken include thornback and blonde rays, cod, pollack, etc.

Due to the very strong tides flowing over the bank, the fish play very heavy when hooked, and it is essential to go equipped with a reasonably strong line (say about 30 to 35lb b.s.), with rod and reel to match. A good selection of heavy leads up to 1½ or 2lb should also be carried. Terminal tackle normally consists of single-hook leger with a 4ft flowing trace below the lead, which is usually attached to a sliding Clements boom.

Favourite bait is a large strip of fresh mackerel. A supply of mackerel can usually be caught on the way out to the fishing mark during the summer months, but it is unwise to rely on this because some days the mackerel shoals are elusive. So play safe and take along an emergency supply of bait – just in case!

25 Portland Race A very dangerous area which should never be fished except by local boatmen with years of experience of the area. Having said this, it is worth mentioning that the Race is a favourite feeding area for big bass, and in suitable weather and tidal conditions local boatmen make some very fine catches. Sometimes I think they are a bit *too* successful, and I cannot help wondering how long it will be before the bass stocks are thinned out.

Lulworth and Adamant Banks Just beyond the E limits of the bay, this area is capable of providing good mixed fishing, with catches of rays, dogfish, black bream, pollack, tope, conger, mackerel and pouting, according to season. This area should only be visited by fair-sized craft possessing a good turn of speed.

Boat Hire

Fishing trips can be arranged through local tackle shops, or with individual boatmen. Weekend trips should be booked well in advance.

Bait and Tackle Dealers

Hayman's Tackle Shop, 13 Trinity Road, Weymouth. Tel: 784786. (Tackle, boat bookings, frozen and live baits)
The Angler's Tackle Store, 64 Part Street, Weymouth. Tel: 782624.
T & M Denning, 114 Portland Road, Wyke Road. Tel: 783145. (Tackle, boat bookings, baits — including live sandeels when available)
Moto-Sails Ltd., 17 St. Edmund Street, Weymouth. Tel: 786710. (Tackle)

Local Baits

(Chart symbols are shown in brackets)

Lugworms (L) can be dug at low tide in the sandflats at the E end of the Fleet, in the Ferrybridge area; also at Castle Cove and Weymouth Sands.

Ragworms (R). Small ragworm, suitable for grey mullet, can be dug at low tide in the Backwater at Weymouth. King ragworm can be bought at Weymouth tackle shops.

Prawns (P) can be netted in the Littlesea near Ferrybridge. Wooden-boomed push-nets are commonly used, but baited drop-nets worked on a moonlit night, or when the water is cloudy, sometimes produce good results. Prawns can also be caught off the ledges at Osmington Mills with drop-nets or metal-framed hand nets. Results are best when the water is dirty.

Slipper Limpets are not really a local bait, but very occasionally they are found on Weymouth beach after an onshore gale.

Local Sea Angling Clubs

There are thriving sea angling clubs at Weymouth and Portland. Details from local tackle shops.

The Chesil Beach

(See also Chart 8, and under **Weymouth and Portland**)

Abbotsbury, Bexington, Swyre, Burton Bradstock

TIDES High Water similar to Bridport.

TOPOGRAPHY For 17 miles, from Chesil Cove to Bridport Harbour, the great shingle ramparts of Chesil Beach stretch unbroken and almost uninhabited. The small fishing-cum-farming villages of Langton Herring. Abbotsbury, Swyre and Burton Bradstock flinch away from the sea; whilst for something like half of its length the beach is cut off from the mainland by a drowned river valley known as the Fleet. Many writers have described the waters of the Fleet as 'landlocked', but in actual fact at Ferrybridge they make direct contact with the tidal waters of Portland Harbour. Bass, mullet and flounders enter the Fleet.

SHORE FISHING

Bass and winter cod are probably the fish most sought after by anglers fishing the Chesil Beach, but they are far from being the species most frequently caught. Whiting, pouting, rays, plaice, dabs and lesser spotted dogfish are much more numerous; whilst spur-dog, bull huss, conger and even turbot may also be encountered, depending on season, weather conditions and section of beach being fished. Also, in calm weather, mackerel are caught by spinning or feathering when the shoals stray close inshore.

For the ground-feeding species either monofil paternoster or leger tackle is suitable. Many anglers favour two hooks, one baited with cuttings of mackerel or sandeel, and the other carrying lugworm, ragworm, slipper limpet or piece of squid.

For details of shore fishing along the eastern end of Chesil Beach, see under **Weymouth and Portland,** Marks 16 and 17.

1 Abbotsbury Beach A road leads down to a longshore car park from Abbotsbury village. Although the beach is of shingle, the sea-bed a little way offshore consists of sand, with patches of shell-grit. Bass, rays and dogfish can be expected when using cuttings of mackerel, squid and whole sandeels. In addition, several fine turbot have been taken from this area, and in late autumn and winter whiting and cod are often present.

During the summer months, from about June until September, shoals of mackerel come close in to this steeply shelving beach, providing excellent sport for the angler equipped with a light casting rod and fixed-spool reel. Some anglers use a trace carrying three feathered hooks, but for maximum sport and excitement it is best to use a light spinning outfit designed to cast a lure in the ½ to 1oz range. A small silver 'Toby' or 'Flectolite' spoon can be relied upon to give good results, and a small German Sprat is also excellent.

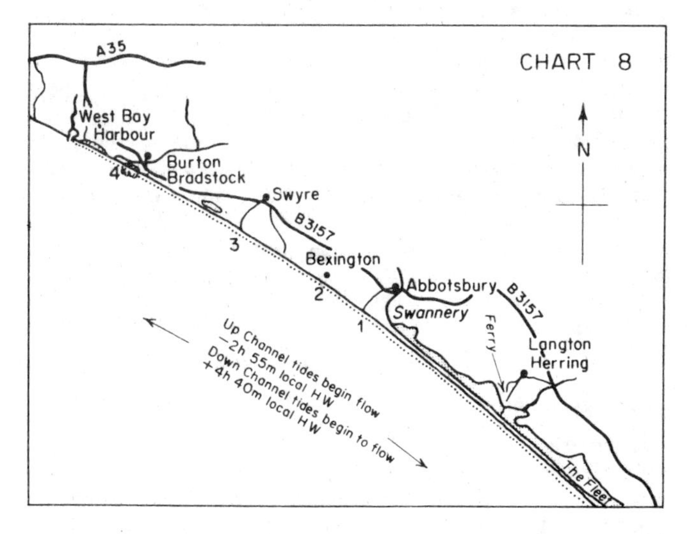

Of course, as mackerel are really fish of the open sea, it is only for comparatively brief spells that the shoals wander within casting distance of the shore. Local anglers, therefore, normally tackle up for this method of fishing only when they know the mackerel are present close inshore.

Often the position of a mackerel shoal can be pinpointed by a tell-tale patch of disturbed water, caused either by the mackerel themselves, or by the whitebait they are hunting. Gulls and terns, wheeling and diving on the whitebait, are another sure indication that mackerel are chasing the small fry from below.

If possible, the bait or lure should be cast slightly ahead and to the far side of the shoal, and retrieved more or less through the centre of it. This is not always easy because mackerel are fast-moving fish, and between casts the angler often has to run along the beach in order to keep pace with the shoal. For this reason he should carry a haversack for the catch, and as little other cumbersome equipment as possible.

2 Bexington Beach This stretch of shore is popular with many anglers because it is easily reached by road, with parking for cars just behind the beach. The fishing is similar to that at Abbotsbury.

3 Cogden Beach Catches similar to Abbotsbury.

4 Burton Freshwater Until a few years ago Burton Freshwater was just a blind river mouth and a name on the map. Nowadays it possesses a sizeable caravan camp, and during the summer months it is one of the most populated places along the Chesil Beach. Bass are sometimes attracted by the fresh water percolating through the shingle; whilst a little to the E an inshore reef, inhabited by prawns and other crustaceans, presents an additional attraction for these fish. It is therefore a good plan to cast out ground tackle as close to these rocks as possible without getting snagged. Conger and pouting can also be expected here. Some of the conger are large, and specimens of over 40lb have been caught on occasions. Nearby Burton Bradstock beach is also fished quite a lot, results being best after dark.

BOAT FISHING

It is possible to launch a boat anywhere along the Chesil Beach *when sea conditions permit*. The shore lies wide open to the SW, however, and more often than not a heavy and dangerous ground swell is running – even in summer. Some open rowing and outboard-powered dinghies are kept on the beach at Abbotsbury, Bexington and Burton Bradstock, but so far as is known, none are let out on hire.

With the exception of the Swyre Ledge and Chesil Cove areas, there are few rock marks along the Chesil Beach. However, some very good black bream are caught at 'the Buoys' and several other marks off Abbotsbury; also dabs, plaice, rays, whiting, cod and occasional turbot and monkfish according to season. Mackerel are plentiful from May to September. Tope are hardly ever fished for by boat anglers working off the Chesil, but are believed to be present in fair numbers within a mile of the shore.

Several useful rock marks can be reached by dinghy from Burton Bradstock beach, and these yield mainly pouting, conger, huss and pollack. Some excellent rays are also found off Burton Freshwater. These marks are described more fully under **Bridport.**

A fair amount of boat fishing is carried on from Chesil Cove, and just S of the cove there are some useful inshore rock marks which yield conger, huss, pollack, pouting and wrasse; with codling in season over broken ground. Boat anglers lacking local knowledge should not venture more than about ¾ mile S of Chesil Cove, as the tide sets with increasing strength towards the dangerous Portland Race.

Bridport (See also Chart 9)

(West Bay and Eype)

TIDES HW: + 4h 27m London Bridge. Rise: 12ft at Springs; 8ft at Neaps. Tidal Streams: Fairly weak, with a maximum speed of just over 1 knot at Springs.

TOPOGRAPHY. The town of Bridport, oddly enough, lies some 2 miles inland, and it is to Bridport's marine suburb of West Bay that holidaymakers flock in summer. It is a small place, with a large caravan camp.

West Bay possesses no spectacular attractions, but the surrounding coastal scenery is good, with golden-hued cliffs stretching away in either direction. The shoreline is shingly, and it is, in fact, the W extremity of the Chesil Beach.

The harbour is unusual, consisting of a rectangular tidal basin connected with the open sea by a long and narrow 'gut' running out through the Chesil Beach between two stone piers. It faces SW, and cannot be used during strong onshore winds, owing to the heavy swell which breaks just inside the entrance. Even in moderate weather the entrance is tricky to negotiate – more so when entering than when leaving.

At low tide the entrance practically dries out, and the harbour is then unusable, with a fierce scour caused by opened river sluices breaking over the bar.

SHORE FISHING

1 East Pier The end of this stone pier is much used by holiday anglers during the summer months, and although a variety of fish are taken, large specimens are few and far between. The locals generally prefer beach fishing, and when they do use the piers it is usually at night. Then, especially in autumn, some good fish nose around the piles, including the occasional bass.

Other fish caught include dabs, plaice, mackerel, scad, pouting, dogfish, conger and small wrasse. Also, I once saw a very good sole taken here, but this was a rather unusual capture. Mullet are also present on occasions, but not many anglers try for them.

2 West Pier This pier is used more by prawners than anglers, but a certain amount of fishing is carried on from the end. Results are said to be slightly inferior to those on the East Pier, but at night there is a fair chance of taking conger. On the outer side of the pier there is snaggy ground.

3 West Beach This is not considered a very good fishing area by the locals, but every year sees a few bass taken here by holiday anglers fishing at night. More often, however, the catch consists of pouting, with the occasional conger and dogfish, Daytime fishing is often impossible during the summer months owing to the crowds of swimmers. There are some snaggy patches, especially towards West Cliff, but it is in this direction that best results are often obtained. A preliminary inspection at low tide is also recommended, preferably from the top of the West Cliffs. One good spot, it will be noted, lies almost below a 'mock Tudor' house.

4 Eype Mouth About a mile W of Bridport Harbour is Eype Mouth – a gap in the cliffs through which flows a small stream, and where a few boats are beached. Eype village, about ¼ mile inland, is a pleasant little holiday resort in its own right. Fishing from the beach at Eype is reasonably good for pouting, conger, dogfish and the occasional bass. The sea-bed is very snaggy, but the use of a spoon-shaped lead and fast-retrieve reel will do much to prevent tackle being lost. The cleanest ground will be found in the immediate vicinity of the gap, but in summer this bit of shore is much used by swimmers. This beach is, in fact, recommended mainly for night fishing, and some good bass (up to 11lb or more) have been taken here after dark.

A two-hook nylon monofil trace is recommended, with the lower hook about 2/0 to 4/0 and carrying a cutting of mackerel, frozen sandeel or squid, and the other hook, smaller and finer in the wire, carrying rag, lug or squid tentacle.

Useful Shore Fishing Reference

Mackerel Spinning. See under **Chesil Beach,** Mark 1.

BOAT FISHING

Most of the boat angling out of Bridport Harbour is carried on over rocky marks, and the catches consist mainly of pouting,

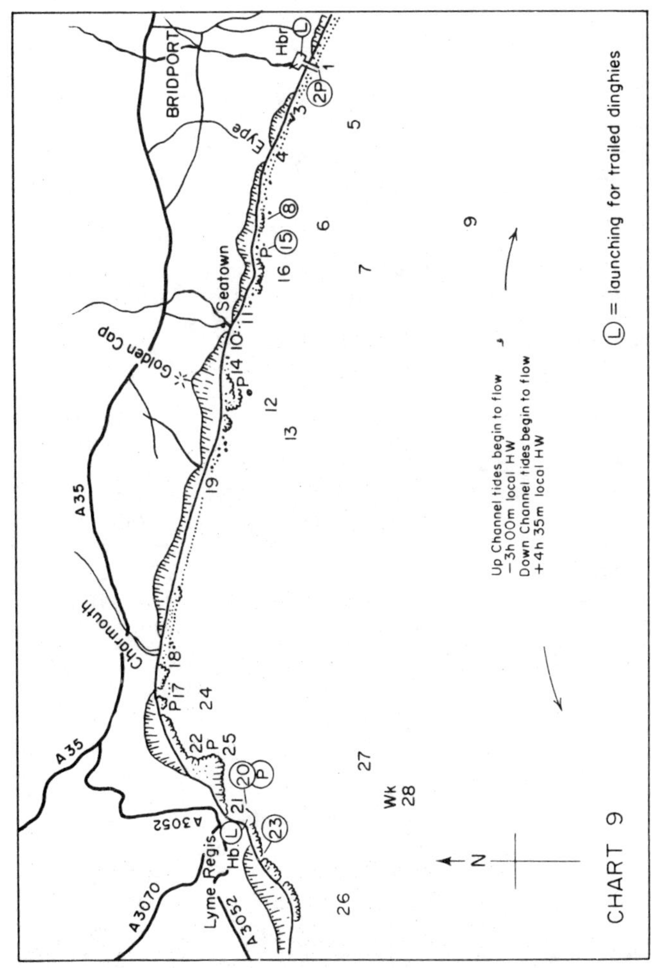

conger, black bream, huss, lesser spotted dogfish, rays, pollack and wrasse, according to the season and the method used. Plenty of mackerel are also caught by trolling and feathering.

There are fairly extensive areas of fine sand and grit where dabs and plaice may be found, although the locals rarely try for them with rod and line.

5 Pollack Grounds This area of rough ground and rocky ridges lies about ¾ mile SW of the harbour entrance, and in summer it is often marked by lobster pot buoys. Pollack, conger, wrasse, huss and pouting are found here; also occasional thornback rays on the outer sandy fringes of the mark. Recommended methods and baits: conger, huss and rays (legering with large cuttings of mackerel or herring); pollack and pouting (driftlining with single hook trace baited with live prawn, large ragworms or mackerel strip); wrasse (as for pollack and pouting, but no fish baits); pollack and mackerel (trolling with spinner or 'Red Gill' sandeel, preferably in early morning or evening. Also feathering from a drifting dinghy).

6 High Ground Another rocky reef, similar to Mark 5, and lying a little more than ½ mile due W of it. When approaching from West Bay, keep the inshore end of West Pier in line with North Hill for 1½ miles, when Eype Rocks, below Thorncombe Beacon, should appear directly abeam.

7 Whiting Grounds This is an area of fine sand where whiting are often found in autumn and winter. To fetch up over this ground, keep Shipton Hill (it looks like a cone with the top cut off) in line with the E end of West Bay promenade until the Anchor Inn, Seatown, is in line with the clump of pines on Langdon Hill. Method: drifting or anchored, using paternoster tackle carrying two or three hooks baited with cuttings of herring, sprat and fresh-caught whiting. Alternatively, use a single hook on a fine monofil trace. Dabs are also found in this area at times.

8 Thorncombe Rocks An extensive reef of tumbled, kelpy boulders extends seawards below the 500ft high cliffs of Thorncombe Beacon, and this is a productive inshore dinghy fishing area. It also offers possibilities for larger craft on those days when strong offshore winds make it impossible for them to fish the more distant deep-sea marks. Slow trolling with a 'Red Gill' plastic sandeel, using oars or a quiet-running inboard engine, will often account for pollack (including some in the 6 to 10lb range) and the occasional bass. Spinning from a drifting dinghy also takes mackerel, pollack, garfish and bass. Driftlining at anchor with a live prawn accounts for pollack, bass and pouting. Legering on sand close to the reef with mackerel strip or squid baits takes conger, huss, pouting and the occasional bass. Light float fishing at anchor, using a small strip of mackerel as bait, takes mackerel, garfish and pollack. Mullet shoals are also present in summer in the rocky coves and inlets, and if a selected area is groundbaited regularly with bread over a period of days the mullet can be tempted to take float fished bread flake, paste or crust on a size 10 or 12 hook.

9 Far Marks There are several areas of rock and rough ground from 2½ to 5 miles offshore. Their exact location is not easy to describe in writing, but they can often be pinpointed during the summer months by the presence of lobster pot buoys. If present, these buoys can usually be located by steering SSW out of West Bay harbour. Legering, deep driftlining and paternostering can produce good results with pouting, black bream, rays, conger, dogfish, pollack and wrasse. Sea conditions can change very quickly and visiting boat anglers are advised to visit these marks with a local boatman. Baits as recommended under Mark 5.

Local Baits
(Chart symbols are shown in brackets)

Prawns (P) can be caught in late summer and autumn off the outer (W) side of the West Pier, using baited drop-nets. The nets must be fitted with long ropes.

Mackerel. Fresh-caught mackerel can often be bought from local boatmen. They can also be caught in season from a dinghy or shore on feathers, spinner or float tackle.

Tackle and Bait Dealers
The Tackle Shop (Lawrie and Hugh Rathbone), West Bay. Tel: Bridport 23475 (Tackle, live and frozen baits, boat bookings)
West Bay Water Sports, George Street, West Bay, Bridport. Tel: 421800.

Local Sea Angling Club
West Bay Sea Angling Club (Details from The Harbour Tackle Shop)

Seatown (See also Chart 9)

TIDES Similar to Bridport.

TOPOGRAPHY Seatown can hardly be called a village, for it consists only of a farm, a pub (the Anchor Inn), and about half a dozen houses and cottages. Set in the mouth of a valley, with rolling downs on either side, this settlement is dwarfed by the impressive cliffs of Golden Cap, the highest point on the south coast.

The shoreline is a mile-long stretch of shingle; while at either end of this beach, beneath Ridge Cliffs to the E and Golden Cap to the W, there are submerged reefs and ledges frequented by many species of fish.

Accommodation in Seatown is very limited, but there are several guest houses in Chideock village, which lies about 1 mile inland. There is also a caravan site.

SHORE FISHING

A running leger or nylon monofil paternoster are the two forms of tackle most often used from the beach, and the fish which can be expected are bass, pouting, huss, lesser spotted dogfish, conger, rays, flatfish and wrasse. Recommended baits include mackerel strip, squid, ragworm and lugworm. Spinning with artificial lures also takes mackerel, bass, pollack and the occasional garfish.

10 West Beach There are numerous snaggy places along this beach, and although the angler is less likely to fall foul of them at high water than at low, the use of streamlined leads is always advisable. It is difficult to give the location of snag-free areas, because the sea-bed close inshore changes after every storm, with rocks becoming covered or uncovered by the shifting shingle. However, the sea-bed for about 100 yards west of the Anchor Inn is usually fairly clear.

'The Rushes' is one of the most rewarding shore fishing areas. It lies about two-thirds of the way along the shingle from Seatown Gap to Golden Cap rocks, but without local knowledge, or a preliminary survey at low spring tide, it is very easy to lose tackle on the submerged rocks which lie close inshore.

11 East Beach Few snags will be encountered for the first 300 yards or so E of Seatown Gap, but there are a few large concrete blocks which are submerged except at dead low water. The beach just under the cliff-edge stile at the top end of the car park is a productive area, and is considered the most likely spot for thornback rays.

Seatown beach (both 10 and 11) shelves very steeply, and in settled weather mackerel shoals sometimes come within 20 yards or so of the shore – particularly around high water, and in the early morning and evening. At such times they can be taken by spinning, as described under **Chesil Beach.** Mark 1.

BOAT FISHING

Only small rowing or outboard-powered boats can be used off Seatown beach. This stretch of shore lies wide open to the prevailing SW winds, and quite often, even in summer, it is impossible to launch a boat through the surf for weeks on end.

12 Golden Cap A reef of weedy rocks extends for about ¾ mile off Golden Cap, into a depth of about 5 fathoms. In this area there are a number of extra large steep-to submerged rocks, which offer better than average fishing. It is impossible to give the marks for all of these, but good results will usually be obtained by keeping the chimney of the Anchor Inn, Seatown, in line with the crest of the road (Furchase Hill) leading from Chideock to Bridport. Drop anchor when directly opposite the most westward patch of shingle beach under Golden Cap.

Pouting are the most common species at this place, but pollack and conger are also plentiful, and quite often the latter run to a good size. In addition, wrasse and huss are taken, with occasional rays, lesser spotted dogfish and monkfish on the outer fringes of the mark. Driftlining and drift-fishing close to the bottom accounts for the pouting, wrasse and pollack, and repeated slow reeling in for about ten turns of the reel often helps to stimulate bites. Paternostering produces pouting and wrasse but not many pollack unless a flowing hook-link is used.

For the conger, huss, rays, etc., a running leger is used; or a nylon monofil paternoster with a flowing lower hook-link if the bottom is very snaggy. Conger have sharp teeth which will bite through the customary nylon hook-link, so strong trot-line snooding is often used instead. This is better than wire, because it allows the bait to work more attractively. Baits: large cuttings of mackerel and herring (conger, huss, rays, pouting); live prawns (bass, pollack, pouting, wrasse, thornback rays); ragworm (pollack, poutings, wrasse, bass).

Plenty of mackerel and pollack are taken in this area by trolling or working a feathered trace.

13 Eight Acres This rocky area lies about a mile off Golden Cap, and is a very good area for pollack, conger, huss, large pouting, wrasse and mackerel. Methods and baits similar to Mark 12. To locate it, head out from Golden Cap until the chimneys of a farmhouse just begin to appear over the top of the cliffs W of Golden Cap. The farm in question can be recognised by a triangular-shaped field situated on the hillside behind it.

14 The Corner This is an area of shallow water on the E side of Golden Cap – the 'corner' being formed by rocks jutting out to sea from the end of the shingle beach. Some large bass often venture in here after dark – probably in search of prawns.

A dinghy angler drifting QUIETLY by moonlight with a live prawn on a long flowing trace stands a fair chance of contacting these bass. The cove is shallow with scarcely any tidal flow, so that very little lead need be used. Sometimes a quiet pull on the oars every few seconds helps matters along.

Float fishing with live prawn is another likely method, yielding pollack as well as the occasional bass.

Bottom fishing here is capable of yielding conger, huss and pouting, but larger specimens will normally be taken at Marks 12 and 13.

15 East Ebb Cove This is another rocky area, lying in a small bay formed by the out-jutting shores of Ridge Cliff and Thorncombe Beacon. There is a fair chance of taking bass by the methods described under Mark 14, and in addition the cove is often visited by shoals of good-sized mullet. They are hardly ever fished for with rod and line, however.

16 Doghouse Point At the E end of Seatown beach the shoreline juts out slightly below the cliffs of Doghouse Hill to form a rocky promontory. In places these rocks extend several hundred yards beyond the low tide line, where they eventually give way to a mixture of sand and gravel. This general area produces conger, huss and thornback rays on mackerel-baited leger tackle. Somewhat closer inshore, anchoring over the reef, good catches of mackerel and garfish can often be taken in summer by driftlining or light float fishing with mackerel strip baits. Similar tactics, but using a live prawn or frozen sandeel as bait, also offers a chance of taking bass.

Local Baits
(Chart symbols are shown in brackets)

Ragworms can be bought at West Bay, 3 miles distant. (See under **Bridport**.)

Prawns (P) can be caught among the rock pools under Golden Cap, either with baited drop-nets or a hand-net. An outgoing tide is best. For preference the water should be cloudy; when it is gin-clear very few prawns will be taken in drop-nets.

Mackerel can often be caught by spinning or feathering from the beach. They can also be caught from a boat by trolling or feathering.

Frozen sandeels can be bought at the Caravan Site shop, Seatown. They make an excellent shore fishing bait for bass and thornback rays.

Limpets are plentiful on the rocks under Golden Cap and Ridge Cliff, but are not recommended except for wrasse.

Charmouth (See also Chart 9)

TIDES Similar to Lyme Regis.

TOPOGRAPHY Although there is some shingle, Charmouth beach consists largely of sand flanked by rocks and tidal pools. The place is therefore very popular with children; particularly as this stretch of shore, and the one at neighbouring Lyme Regis, are the only sandy beaches to be found along this coast for something like 20 miles in either direction.

For this reason the shore becomes rather crowded at weekends in the holiday season, but it is usually possible to find a reasonably quiet fishing spot by walking some distance W along the beach.

SHORE FISHING

17 West Beach A preliminary inspection at low tide is recommended before fishing this beach. It will then be possible to cast out on to sandy ground flanked by rocks. One good area will be found some distance along towards Black Ven, where an outcrop of blue lias discolours the water. From here some good bass have been taken, usually after dark. Pouting and conger can also be expected. Leger tackle seems to do best, and useful baits are large cuttings of mackerel, frozen herring or squid, king ragworm, lugworm and prawns. Do not leave the bait lying too long in one place, but slowly reel in two or three feet of line every minute or so.

18 Groyne Beach This spot is almost impossible to fish on a crowded day in summer, but after sundown, when things are quieter, there may be quite good sport. Though the foreshore is mainly sandy, the sea-bed below low tide level is rocky. There is, however, a narrow sandy channel between the rocks, just W of the groyne, and immediately in front of a longshore building with a cone-shaped roof. Tackle and baits similar to those recommended for Mark 17 do well here, and the ability to cast out a good way with accuracy is often an advantage. Even when there are no crowds, night fishing is definitely best.

19 St Gabriel's Beach This beach of mixed shingle and small near-shore rocks lies under the cliffs about 2 miles E of Charmouth Gap. It can be reached by walking along the foreshore, except around high water, when at several places the sea may be washing right up to the base of the cliffs.

Alternative routes are along the main road as far as Morecombelake, and then down the lane that leads to St. Gabriel's Farm; or on foot up Stonebarrow Lane and along the cliff-top – a grand walk. St. Gabriel's Beach is finally reached by a footpath that descends through a gap in the cliffs in company with a small waterfall.

Because of its lonely situation this beach is seldom fished, but an evening expedition here often produces surprises. Anglers using fish bait after dark have taken bass, skate, conger and pouting; whilst several really large monkfish have also been caught – usually at night during the summer months, when these weird-looking fish come close inshore to give birth to their living young.

The sea-bed is snaggy in many places, but a spoon-shaped lead and fast retrieve will help to prevent loss of tackle. The beach about 250 yards W of the cascade is recommended, where an outcrop of yellowish gravel appears in the cliff.

BOAT FISHING

Although a few dinghies suitable for inshore fishing are kept on Charmouth Beach, the shore itself is not particularly convenient. It is rather a long drag down to the water's edge at low tide, and the crowded nature of the beach in summer does not make matters any easier.

Normally it is better to take a boat out from Lyme Regis harbour, which lies less than 2 miles distant across the bay. Boat fishing marks for the Charmouth area will therefore be found under **Lyme Regis.**

Local Baits

(Chart symbols are shown in brackets)

Lugworm (L) can be dug at low tide W of Black Ven in sandy areas where the worm casts are thickest.

Prawns (P) can be netted among rock pools to the W of Charmouth Beach. They can also be taken off Black Ven Ledges by using baited drop-nets from a dinghy.

Lyme Regis (See also Chart 9)

TIDES HW: + 4h 50m London Bridge. Rise: 12ft at Springs; 9ft at Neaps. The tidal streams offshore are weak, with a maximum speed of approximately 1 knot.

TOPOGRAPHY The outstanding feature of this pleasant, modest-sized holiday resort is the picturesque semi-tidal harbour known as the Cobb. Tucked into a 'corner' of the coastline, and backed by steep hills, small craft find welcome shelter here from strong W winds. At such times, inshore fishing is often possible from Pinhay Cliffs to Black Ven when it is impossible everywhere else along the coast as far as Portland.

The general setting of Lyme Regis, with its encircling amphitheatre of cliffs, makes it a wonderful little suntrap. The beach is sandy and clean, and the bathing is safe.

The motorist-angler trailing his own dinghy can launch into the harbour without difficulty, but first contact the harbour master. Details of launching fees are displayed on a notice board. There is a car park immediately behind the launching place, but it quickly fills up in summer.

SHORE FISHING

20 The Cobb The stone quay of Lyme Regis harbour, known as the Cobb, is used by many visiting anglers. The catches are not spectacular by day due to the amount of boat traffic, but late evening and after-dark fishing yields pollack (some, on occasions, surprisingly large), pouting, bass, wrasse and conger. Bottom fishing is possible in sandy areas, but the sea-bed is mainly rocky, and float gear is most commonly used. Float-spinning with ragworm bait will take pollack when high water coincides with the last hour or two of daylight.

Dabs are sometimes caught by casting out light leger tackle from the detached wall immediately N of the harbour entrance.

21 Cobb Gate Beach This sandy beach stretches between the harbour and the rocky outcrop known as Lucy's Ledge. It is reputed to be a useful place for bass, but results have been disappointing in recent years. Daylight fishing is often impossible during the holiday season as the beach is much used by swimmers, but in any case fishing is only really worthwhile after dark. Best results are usually obtained by casting out leger tackle onto sand as near as possible to Lucy's Ledge. Baits: cuttings of mackerel or squid; lugworm, large ragworm.

22 The Spittles This stretch of shoreline lies 'just around the corner' from Lyme's main holiday beaches, below some sombre-hued cliffs of blue lias. At first glance it looks a rather forbidding fishing spot, with a strata of blue lias bedrock sloping gently seawards, and with innumerable scattered boulders waiting to trap your tackle.

Nevertheless, it is excellent bass country, and provided you pick your casting area carefully at dead low tide, it is usually possible to lob the bait on to a patch of smooth blue lias among the boulders. There's no need to cast out a long way – 30 to 40 yards is plenty far enough to reach the feeding bass after dark on a flooding tide.

The sea in this area is nearly always coloured by the local blue lias deposits, and for this reason it is a useful spot for daylight fishing. Nevertheless, like every other beach along this coast, best results are generally obtained at dusk or after dark – preferably during the first two or three hours of the flood tide.

23 Western Beach This beach extends westwards of Lyme Harbour for about half a mile, after which the shoreline becomes progressively more rocky as one travels towards Seven Rock Point. Below the half-tide line the beach immediately W of the harbour consists mainly of clean sand interspersed with low-lying rocky ledges. Above the half-tide line there is a bank of shingle. Due to the complex nature of this shoreline it is essential to make a preliminary survey at low tide before risking your tackle.

Bass frequent this stretch of beach, and best results are usually obtained when a groundswell or moderate onshore wind is creating some surf. However, plenty of good bass have also been captured during flat calm conditions.

One productive spot lies near Poker's Pool, a rocky area with sand gullies about half a mile west of the harbour. Because of its numerous snags it is not much fished, but its bass potential is far better than most visiting anglers suspect. As a point of interest, the county boundary runs through this shore mark, and on one evening fishing visit I had the novel experience of hooking an 8¼ lb bass in Devon waters, and beaching it in Dorset!

BOAT FISHING

24 Canary Ledges From the cliffs immediately W of Charmouth a submerged ledge of weedy rock stretches over ¼ mile out to sea, and in places is almost awash at low Springs. Around the outer limits of this ledge there is 'scrubby' ground, with some largish rocks under a fathom or two of water. Here quite often will be found reasonably good inshore fishing – the species most commonly caught being pouting, conger, pollack, wrasse and huss. All these are taken while fishing at anchor; but over a wider area of the ledge, and off nearby Black Ven, pollack, mackerel and bass are also to be had by trolling. The bass are mostly taken when trolling quietly with oars, using a plastic sandeel.

Alternatively, drifting around the ledge and Black Ven with a live prawn on a flowing trace will often account for bass and pollack. This is usually best on a calm evening, or shortly after dark.

Yet another rewarding method is driftlining from an anchored boat. This will take most of the species already mentioned, according to the fishing depth and bait used. Baits: large cuttings of mackerel and herring (conger, huss, rays, pouting); live prawns (bass, pollack, pouting, wrasse, thornback rays); ragworm (pollack, pouting, wrasse, bass).

25 Broad Ledge. This ledge of rock extends E from St. Michael's Church tower, and although rarely producing large fish, it offers a reasonable chance of sport when strong W winds are producing rough conditions farther out in the bay. The fishing methods and species caught are similar to Mark 23. The water is rather shallow, and best results are usually obtained near the outer fringes of the ledge, when the water is cloudy.

26 Pinhay Rocks This mark lies about 2 miles SW of Lyme Regis harbour, about ¾ mile offshore. It is good for pouting, conger, pollack, wrasse, huss, etc. To reach it, keep Charmouth Gap just open of the Cobb wall until Pinhay Bay is abeam. A driftline fished deep does well here, particularly if the bait is fished sink and draw. For ground-feeding species try leger tackle, or a two-hook nylon monofil paternoster with the lower hook on a flowing trace. Baits: prawns, ragworm, squid, mackerel or herring cuttings.

The stretch of coast from the Cobb to Pinhay Bay is often a good area for mackerel. They are taken by trolling, or by working a feathered trace while trolling slowing or drifting with the tide.

27 Outer Marks There are several useful boat marks a mile or two offshore from Lyme. Their precise location is difficult to describe in writing, however, and they are best visited with a local boatman. Catches include conger, huss, rays, pollack, pouting and flatfish by all the usual methods. Mackerel are usually plentiful in summer, and are a favourite hook bait for most of the species mentioned, with the exception of flatfish, which are mostly taken on worm baits.

28 The Wreck A sunken wreck lies about 1 ½ miles due S of the Cobb. There is good general fishing here, but local knowledge is needed to pinpoint the mark. Large strips of fresh-caught mackerel do well on a running leger, or a driftline fished 'deep and steep'.

Golden Cap Many boat anglers from Lyme Regis visit the marks off Golden Cap. Details of these will be found in the section dealing with **Seatown.**

BOAT HIRE

Fishing trips can be arranged with local boatmen.

Local Baits
(Chart symbols are shown in brackets)

Prawns (P) can be caught with baited drop-nets from the stone pier at the harbour entrance, or by hand-netting among weedy and sand-fringed tidal rocks. However, better catches will be obtained as a rule by working baited drop-nets from a dinghy along suitable stretches of shore. The Spittles area is sometimes productive, but when the water is clear here better results will usually be obtained off Black Ven, a promontory of blue lias just W of Charmouth.

Mackerel can be caught in the bay during the summer months by trolling or feathering from a dinghy. Also, they are often obtainable from local boatmen.

Tackle Dealers

Lyme Leisure, 26 Broad Street, Lyme Regis. Tel: 2948 (Tackle, baits, boating wear, etc.)

The Tackle Box, Bosun's Yard, Marine Parade, Lyme Regis. Tel: (0404) 850109.